Laurie A Wondra

EMERGING ENERGY

A Journey Within

ISBN: 0615536875
ISBN-13: 9780615536873

Dedication

This book is dedicated to all on this wonderful journey of life. It is our collective energy that makes this journey amazing.

Acknowledgements

To my children, Jake and Em, who have been on this journey with me since their births. You are my joy, my pride, and my love for you is beyond words. To my friends in Sedona who have taught, validated and helped me stretch beyond what I thought possible. To my family and friends in Minnesota, who watched and assisted as my dream emerged to reality. Love to you.

Contents

Contents

Introduction

We all have gifts, but for me, they are my intuition, my ability to channel angels and speak with those that have crossed over, my knowledge and work with rainbow light, and energy.

My first memories are as early as grade school, but I spent considerable amounts of time not understanding and then later suppressing these gifts. I hated funerals, movies about haunted houses, or ghosts. I could not sit through a scary movie without having a pillow in front of my face, because I could feel all that was happening on the screen and had a beyond-movie-plot-knowing of what was going to happen next. I grew up in a Catholic household, went to a Catholic school, and went to church multiple times during the week. Anything we were not able to explain was put in the hands of God. I went to sleep with the covers drawn over my head for years, putting life into the hands of God. Over the years, I had friends that came in and out of my life that were much like me, closet "dabblers." We questioned, explored, and then retreated in fear if we could not explain something. I was drawn to books by James Van Praagh and caught all the John Edward TV shows. I was almost convinced to take a class about ghost hunting by Echo Bodine but, out of fear, never signed up. I had long been told I was a healer and an intuitive, but if someone told me back then that I'd be channeling and talking to energies, I would have been too petrified to say anything.

Much like many of us run from change or challenges in our lives, I was running from something I did not understand. I was running from my purpose, my natural gifts. I was running from me, but I did not know that. The running for me showed up in *doing*. I was very good at *doing*. I had worked in information technology for more than twenty-five years, and over that time, I moved up the corporate ladder. I'd also gotten married, had two children, and had a beautiful home and a strong circle of friends. What more could I want?

As I got older, and one would say wiser, I began to have a stronger sense that something greater than me was urging me to explore. My problem was I did not know what to explore. I had this extreme gnawing to do something, find something, be something, but I could not put my finger on exactly what I was supposed to be doing. The statement about "doing what you love and the money will come" did not compute for me. Money doesn't just magically come; you have to *work* for it. You have to be successful. You have to have goals, direction, and a vision, blah, blah, blah. Where was this longing coming from?

My "ah-ha" moment came on a family trip, over Easter, when we went to Sedona, Arizona. I might say this was the boiling point or the strongest moment of saying out loud, "ENOUGH." Something within me that day popped. I did not know where I was headed, but I certainly knew that I was done with a lot that was not working. That something that popped was enough to push me forward and take new steps in my life. Though the searching and the desire for change had been there for years, this time there was something greater behind the urge for something different. I spent the next year doing much soul work, heart work, and physical and emotional work to *wake up*. I began to feel younger. My thinking was clear. I walked with a smile on my face, laughter came easy, and I found purpose. I found direction.

What I have learned on this journey must be shared. This book has been bubbling to come out, and now it is here. My lessons and learnings are repeatable. I reflect and marvel at how dramatically my life has changed, how my beliefs have grown and expanded, and what I now understand about self and who I AM. My lessons carry over into how I am in my relationships with my family, friends, coworkers, clients, and everyone who steps into my life. I wish I would have read my book twenty-five years ago. I wish someone had given me this information and the method to inspire and move me along quicker and with fewer deviations to my path. I am grateful for the discovery of my gifts and how those gifts can assist others that I meet, and it is my desire to share this with you.

We are moving into a time when we must get out of the head and into the heart. As the economy continues to teeter from stability to instability, as relationships are tested all around us, and as the next generations step into the work force, it is important to quickly move through the transition so that we can *be*.

There are events happening around the globe that are new, and many of us do not understand how to handle them. We are exposed to situations that we do not understand, yet we are forced to act. We have endings and beginnings with careers, marriages, and deaths that leave us to question why and what is next. We are overwhelmed, depressed, bored, tired, and lack engagement with our inner being. Many of us have given up. Our earth is rebelling with storms, earthquakes, fires, and people in rage. Energy is moving on our planet, but most do not know how to handle it. Those that understand this energy do not know what do with it.

My travels, quiet time, practices, experiences, and learning were the doors to who I AM. I chose to walk through that door to clarity and understanding. I invite you to share with me my learnings and lessons with the intent to show all that commit to a better "being."

Blessings and love to all.

Chapter 1: I AM

Knowing Me

I have worked as an executive in the field of information technology (IT) for almost thirty years. By most belief systems, I am in a left-brained career as shown in Figure 1.

Left Brain	Right Brain
Logical	Random
Sequential	Intuitive
Rational	Holistic
Analytical	Synthesizing
Objective	Subjective
Look at parts	Look at the whole

Figure 1: Left Brain/Right Brain[1]

My background in IT is really about what I do and where I do it... most of the time. There is more to me than that functional title. The title really does not tell you who I am or anything about ME. You may know me by my name, by my face, or through an acquaintance and therefore have a mechanism to identify me. Based on your perception of my presentation to you, you know me. The fact is you do not really know me but rather a presentation of me. Most people do not know themselves deeply. They are walking heads that interact with each other every day. We interact based on perceptions of each other and how we think we are. Looking at me, you know nothing of the journey I

---

1   http://www.funderstanding.com/content/right-brain-vs-left-brain.

have been on or what has brought me to find the importance of my experiences so that they can help you to further your journey. Though I am a corporate executive, I am also an intuitive reader and energy healer.

If I look at the figure above, I can operate in both domains. In my IT career, I am all the attributes listed under the left-brain list. I can be logical, sequential, or any of the other attributes listed. I am, however, also the characteristics listed for the right brain (intuitive, holistic, etc.). When I focus and am aware, I can use attributes from both lists.

If I took an industry-standard test of my style, I would be identified a "Driver" and have the qualities of the left-brain list. When I have taken these sorts of tests, they are work related and call out how I am with teams. Most often the tests are taken in the context of an environment or a situation. In the Myers-Briggs Type Indicator (MBTI), which is based on theories extrapolated from the work of Carl Jung, communication is broken into four opposite parings, with sixteen possible psychological types, as shown in Figure 2:

ESTJ: Extraversion (E), Sensing (S), Thinking (T), Judgment (J)
INFP: Introversion (I), Intuition (N), Feeling (F), Perception (P)

Myers-Briggs

Dichotomies

Extroversion (**E**)	(**I**) Introversion
Sensing (**S**)	(**N**) Intuition
Thinking (**T**)	(**F**) Feeling
Judgment (**J**)	(**P**) Perception

Figure 2: Myers-Briggs Types

In this test, I would be categorized as an INTJ: Introvert, Feeling, Thinking, and Judging. This test would show that I am also both right and left brain. However, this is still not who I am. Though I am a "do-er" at home, and my children would say I rarely sit, there is more crossover of the dichotomies. My son would say that I am extroverted and I love people, but my preference is not to be on center stage with large groups. I prefer smaller intimate groups where I can get to know people more personally. It is not to say that I will not present to large groups or teams of large groups, but if I operated from my preference at all times, it would be one on one with individuals. I like the camaraderie of team sports and group activities but tend to focus on one or a few areas during an event.

Many of us create our external presentation of self based on who we think we should be, what we want to be, or how others project who we should be. We create a portion of ourselves for specific situations; being a manager, parent, or spouse requires us to develop certain strengths. Somewhere in our history, we have lost, or perhaps have not understood, who we are. Most people can wear a persona for a given amount of time, but at some point, it becomes uncomfortable and they must shed it. Many people adapt or shift personas frequently during their lives and may even say they have never felt comfortable in their own skin. They may live a life filled with shifting behaviors or styles, never becoming comfortable. Being on "the right seat" means understanding yourself, and that often means admitting that you are on the wrong seat or even on the wrong bus.

When we develop a persona based on what is perceived that others want us to be, we get confused. When we develop a persona based on what we believe will please another person we get lost. If with each interaction we continue to adjust based on either of these, we never allow the other person to see our true being. This behavior is not comfortably sustainable.

Our kids are distracted by their iPod, Wii, Xbox, and other electronic gadgets that perpetuate the avoidance of self or the understanding of internal being. We have become social only in the sense of Facebook or other social networks, and many in the technology and marketing field state that this creates opportunities to reach people and sell.

This book is about going within and understanding self from an I AM versus I DO standpoint. It is a celebration of how the individual spirit contributes to the events of each day. It is how you feel along this journey and how you participate in others lives and how they feel. It is about self, emotions, actions, and knowing who you are so that you can be happy and complete along this journey. Because we live in a society where we interact with others who are also on their journey, it is only fitting that we understand ourselves, which helps others understand themselves.

How I Got Here

We live in a fast-paced, Western world where *doing* and results are expected. Faster and higher output is assumed to mean better. In the industrial age, for manufacturers this meant more profit. More profit meant faster and higher output, and the cycle continued. I grew up in the Midwest with parents whose work ethic meant long hours, hard work, and results. I often heard that success requires hard work. "Hard work" equated to longer hours or more output. As a child, to sit meant that I was not *doing* anything, and that was unacceptable. To always be productive or producing results meant always doing something that had tangible results.

Baby boomers grew up in a time where there were no electronic distractions such as computers, MP3 players. Television broadcasting was limited to a few channels. Most of our day was left to be filled, and we always found something to do. Doing was a way of life, and there was little discussion of how we felt. Goals were "what do you want to *do* when you grow up," not "how you want to *BE* when you grow up."

Though social well-being was introduced, emotional intelligence, emotional well-being, and emotional health were not well-known terms until recently. When I was in my late teens, I bought a book about higher consciousness and our higher beings. Without much explanation I felt a clear understanding deep within my core, but there was no community to discuss those beliefs. Much of that work was considered voodoo, hooey, "fluffy touchy-feely work," and not necessary to be productive in the business or manufacturing world. We were a society of "putting in time to get results."

Corporations began to look at the hiring process to be inclusive of community involvement and social well-being rather than strictly academic and job history. Some hiring practices required psychological testing, and tests were developed to assess how well rounded a potential candidate was. Hiring became more about adaptability, aptitude, and social understanding, with the belief that if that foundation was there, the skills for the job could be learned. Many college students now plan extracurricular activities around social volunteering and ways to demonstrate leadership and cultural knowledge.

In our fast-paced lives, we are driven by "throughput" or output, by a desire to quickly "check the box" and move on to the next activity. We rarely stop to celebrate or even assess what we just experienced beyond the tangible result. In the language of continuous process improvement, what is needed could be called "six-sigma for the soul" and "continuous improvement for the spirit."

Most people fill their days with doing. Time spent on computers, watching television, or spending energy on events or items that do not pertain to them are not deemed important.

I worked hard, played hard, and lived in a fast-paced world. I do not have much downtime, but that was by design. Whether I knew it or not, I created a world where I was always busy doing. I believed that my best work was done when I immersed myself in my job. Hours, days, weeks, months flew by, and I would realize that I had missed an entire summer or Christmas season. Coordination of events outside this busyness was painful and often created its own level of stress. Family and friends could not understand why I was busy, but they also were on this same path of busyness. I found myself lost when gathered with friends and they were immersed in conversations about the latest television shows, award shows, or current news. I depended on friends to tell me about world events. The external environment did not seem important, because I was so immersed in doing, throughput, and results. When I spoke with my friends, the conversation went something like this:

"Hi, how are you?"

"Crazy busy, I don't know where the days go."

"I know what you mean. It seems like I can never get ahead of my to-do list."

I thought that I was well organized, and I was being productive, but my life was "crazy busy." I look back on my life and wonder how I did that. My kids have stated that they do not want to lead the type of busy life that they saw me lead.

Throughout my career, I always found or created my jobs that required dedication above and beyond reasonable hours. I was the "Type A" employee who juggled many responsibilities and thrived on action. I would work myself crazy and then needed to hide to reenergize. I never took the time to find what reenergized me, and when I look back, I wonder if I was ever really energized and fully charged or running half-empty all the time.

After many business meetings, dinners, and events, I found myself assessing how I *was*. Who was I presenting myself as? How do I want to be perceived? Who am I? Where did I lose *me*? I had become a "talking head."

There is "busy with tangible outcomes," and there is "busy with no outcome." That busy is centered on computers, television, and time spent with external influences that allow us to avoid our own internal selves. There is "busy from doing" and the feeling that time must be filled with activities tied to results, goals, or getting somewhere. Both are distractions from truly who we are, and they detract us from our purpose in life, or they fill the void when we feel our desired purpose is unobtainable. Millions of people ask themselves every day, "Is this all there is?"

Identity

Many introductions begin with I AM—these two words define our core. They are powerful words that we take for granted each time we introduce ourselves with *I am.*

We live in a culture that is defined by name and title. We are taught that sturdy handshakes, eye contact, and a strong voice are important when we meet or greet someone.

Who are you?

When you say, "Hi, my name is (insert name) and I am (insert title)," how do you present yourself to the world? What is your thirty-second elevator speech? Is that who you are, or is it a snippet of what you want the world to believe about what you do or are doing?

Often when I am introduced to people, they provide their name and title. If I do not know what the title means, I make an assumption. I go to the "title data bank" in my brain and assign a piece of reference material to the person. If there was no time to ask questions or get to know the person or what she did, the easy reference process worked well for me. It was a quick label to attach so when I saw this person again I would have that information. We do that with many other things such as eyes, hair, and type of dress. All these are methods that our brain uses to classify and archive information about the experience of meeting someone new.

In a fast-paced world, titles bring a sense of accomplishment and signal what we have done. They can sometimes be roadmaps to where we are going or who we should align with. Sales organizations spend considerable amount of time assessing decision makers, and the starting point is often a title within an organization. Titles become part of identity. If you have been introduced to someone and you had no idea what his title meant, you probably made something up. Everyone has to 'do' something, and that title becomes their identity.

When mothers (or fathers) quit the workforce to stay home and take care of their children, having no title is often their biggest struggle.

I challenge you to pick a day or a week and pay attention to how often you say or hear these words: "Hi, my name is (insert name) and I am (insert title)."

With titles or labels, we have a perception of how that person acts. Lawyer, policeman, doctor, flight attendant, accountant, manager are just a few examples. These identify what the individual does but not who she is.

Many people *are* their identity. They relate solely to their title as if it were a badge of honor or, in itself, a list of their lifelong accomplishments. Perceptions of what or who they should be are centered on this title, and their image or self-worth can be challenged or crumble if that identity is removed. This may happen with a change of career or loss of a job.

People build stories about their identity. They get locked into ruts or an image versus what or who they intend to be. The identity may have been forced upon them or directed at them as a child, as overbearing parents project what a child should be when he grows up. I searched for that answer to that big question, "What do you want to do?" My parents lovingly tried to direct me to follow the classes and career path that earned the most and cost the least in time and college funds. I grew up in a generation where college was a means of getting onto the earning field as quickly as possible. It was not an "experience" or a life choice but simply related to work. It did not matter if I did not love the work; it was all about earning money and spending it. Today, as I drive to work and sit in traffic, looking at the blank eyes of the other drivers, I wonder how many people are simply going to work to earn a paycheck. They have checked out of the world and are on autopilot as they go to the office or the factory and put in their time. My online friends post comments like, "Is it Friday yet," "Can't wait for the weekend," or "Thank god it's the weekend." I marvel at the amount of time we spend wishing for our time off. What is that telling us? We ought to be focusing on what we like to do, not spending time and energy on things we do not like.

When my son finished his junior year in high school, and he got A's in the courses he loved and almost failed the course he hated. He needed that course to graduate from high school. In this situation he really didn't have a choice. While many of us *do* have choices in life, we remain numb or locked into actions that do not feel comfortable or right. Are we accepting what we have for the sake of survival, a paycheck, clothing, or something else?

When you introduce yourself, think about who you are and how you got to that point. Next, think about if you like being where you are. Ask the question, "How do I define who I AM?"

Many books have been written on setting and obtaining financial growth, achieving success, and other career-based topics. There are books that promise to help us get on the fast track, get to the end game quicker, while skipping over roadblocks. These books are to help us "sprint to the finish line" and forego the journey. There are books that help us find the perfect relationship or the perfect partner, and books that help us understand diversity in our cultures, our communities, and our families. Many books help the readers attract good things into their lives and identify when they attract items that are not on target with what they want. The books include quick methods to "correct course" and move toward life-long goals. There are even books on finding our goals and our purpose and books that helping us through major life transitions.

While many of these books focus outward rather than on the internal, many do discuss the importance of approaching life from a foundation and understanding of self. We are who we are, but do you *know* who you are? Are you comfortable with who you are, and if so, do you wonder what is next? Are you looking for something new? In either case, you have to know yourself.

Understanding I AM and Who I AM Really Is
Identity can be one that we have assigned for ourselves, or it may be one that you have adapted, based on external influences. In either case, it becomes our truth of who we are. This is our I AM. We may find that the identity we assign to ourselves or the identity others assign to us does not fit, and we may find ourselves saying the following:
"I can't live up to anyone's expectations."
"I never feel right."
"I don't know what anyone expects of me."
"I don't know who I'm supposed to be anymore."

These statements demonstrate a conflict between outer and inner belief systems. An identity that we have adapted, that is not pure to our internal identity, will feel out of balance. We continue to act and create events to maintain a false identity, but we never truly feel fulfilled with our internal self. The importance of knowing who I AM is to know self and live with your own assignment of self, not that of an external influence.

Many people search externally for purpose. They ask, "What is my purpose in life? What am I supposed to be doing?" I often see clients who ask that question and see it stated in terms of pain. The client is struggling to feel direction, to fit in the world, and to find happiness. Many do not feel engaged, as if they are not living life to its fullest. They often say they can feel a change, it feels so close they can "almost taste it", but just cannot seem to get what they are supposed to be doing. They only know that what is happening in their life is not enough and they are looking for more.

If you read the above paragraph and you say, "I can relate," you too believe that "there is more," but what is it? To understand how to fill that need, you need to understand yourself and what created the void.

I use the term "Center of Resource Energy" or CORE to describe the center that drives our being. It gets us up and moving in the morning. It is an internal engine that needs fuel just like any other engine. The fuel for CORE is based on I AM. Knowing your I AM allows you to define your fuel and move. If you do not know your true "I AM," you put the wrong fuel in your tank. You run slowly and feel that you always have to be on the move to be continually energized. You are always "hungry."

You might seek events or activities that temporarily put fuel in your tank, and when you run empty, you seek the same or similar activities again. These may manifest as addictions to food, alcohol, drugs, work, drama, and many other areas. Your body and mind are telling you that you do not yet understand I AM.

To fuel your CORE, know what you run on, and find the I AM.

Do-er or Be-er
I once took extended time off before starting a new job. This was not like taking time off when having a baby, taking time off for medical recovery, or being without work and searching for a new position. I intentionally chose to take time away from work and other activities to rest, explore, and get caught up on items that had been placed on the "too-hard" or the "to-do" pile over the years.

I found conversations with people odd. Many did not believe that I was not jumping straight to my next position. That was how they knew me—throughout my life, I always had two careers at the same time, three if you counted being a parent. I was the do-er who juggled life, career, kids, and all the activities that came with these. Why would I take time away from the "normal me"? People did not know how to act around me or what questions they could or should ask.

People asked me what I had been doing. At times, I felt that the conversation was strained, as I felt that I needed to justify my time. At the end of the day, I reflected on all that I had accomplished and felt awesome as my to-do list shrank. I found that this time was the greatest gift the universe gave me and the greatest gift I gave to myself.

During my first week at home, I watched TV for about ten minutes but felt that I was "unproductive." There was no tangible output, nothing to show how I had spent my day. I quickly got into a routine: up with the kids in the morning, breakfast with my daughter, throw a load of clothes in the washer, drive her to school on my way out, get home in time to wake my son, chat with him while he ate his breakfast, and send him off to school. The house was spotless, and I had someone that came on a regular basis to clean the house (she scolded me for pre-cleaning). It was winter in Minnesota, and regular snows kept me busy. My driveway and sidewalks were always clear. I even continued clearing down the sidewalk into my neighbor's domain if I felt overly zealous that day. I started shoveling the deck on a regular basis. My neighbors thought I was crazy. All of it was "something to do."

By week three, all the closets, cabinets, and cupboards where cleaned, organized, and lined with pretty shelf liner. The carpets had been cleaned, and I would have washed windows if it hadn't been winter. By week five, the interior of the house was painted, and the kitchen countertops had been replaced. All my lists were complete. I had done all my doing, and then it happened. It hit me like a lightning bolt. What in the world was I going to do for the next ten weeks? I had two trips planned. One was a family trip to Sedona and the second trip was flying my parents to my sister's home in California. Other than those trips, my list was complete.

Chapter 1: I AM

On my trip to Sedona, I played event planner for my family. I had done research on the Internet, asked friends, and was ready for a fun-filled, packed vacation. The plans included a hiking tour with Mark Griffon with Sedona Mystical Tours, a guide that has since become a dear friend, and I have come to call "Indiana Griffon" The schedule looked like this:

Day 1: Arrive late—check in, dinner, find the pool, swim
Day 2: Drive along Oak Creek, lunch in Flagstaff, take scenic route on return to Sedona checking out landmarks along the way. Evening swim.
Day 3: Morning tour with private guide to experience Sedona. Evening shopping.
Day 4: See Indian ruins and visit artist community in Jerome.
Day 5: Go to Grand Canyon.
Day 6: Shop and pack. Drive to airport. Go home.

It was *doing* a vacation. On Day Two, we argued about where to eat, and there was nothing relaxing about that conversation. If you have ever argued on a vacation, you understand that feeling in your gut. Any feelings of relaxation quickly vanish, and it feels like you are starting all over again to gain a foundation of calmness. We all agreed to "chill out" and start fresh the next morning.

Day Three was wonderful. It was Easter Sunday and warm and sunny. I was worried if the kids were enjoying themselves, and by the looks on their faces, they were not. My daughter had come down with a cold and was hiking with a Kleenex box in hand. It was unseasonably hot in Sedona at that time, and the kids were not happy about going from 20 degree weather in Minnesota to 90 degree weather in Arizona. That evening as I looked at my Day Four activities, it hit me. I was still DOING, and everyone else just wanted to BE. I ripped up the list. We spent Days Four, Five, and Six hanging out. That was tough for me, but it was a beginning. The morning we left Sedona I sat on our patio, journaling, and I wanted to cry. I was not ready to leave, but I did not exactly know why. Why was I crying over leaving a vacation spot? In all the traveling I had done around the world, and all the family vacations, I had never felt this way. I realized at that moment that there was something to learn from being in Sedona and I needed to return to Sedona, alone. I launched onto the speedway of life, body, soul, spirit, and transformation.

When I stopped thinking of *doing* as my purpose in life and began to look at my internal energy, *my* I AM emerged.

Who Do I Want to BE Versus Who I AM

"What do you want to be when you grow up?" Think back to your youth and how many times you were asked that question. Do you remember feeling any panic following that question? Parents often qualify with statements such as "I do not care what she does, I just want her to be happy." Such statements, though important, begin to direct us down the path of being a do-er early in life.

We grow up and approach life with a focus on output, throughput, action, and results. This puts a tremendous amount of pressure on us in our youth. Students know little about the selection of a career, nor what a person in a particular career "does." Does it sound good? Does it sound fun? We coach and approach life from a DO-ing aspect with little or no thought in how we want to be.

In the workplace, bonuses and compensation are generally assessed and distributed based on what we have done or will plan to do. Corporations assess talent around doing and deliverables. Career development is based on what you want to do in future years. These are all necessary for businesses to run effectively. They are driven by tangible results and easier to measure than asking someone "how they want to be next year."

Generation X-ers and Y-ers have different expectations than baby boomers. My son has told me for many years that he does not want to work as hard as I do. His priorities are fun, friends, and a life outside a structured office. There is information readily available to help our kids decide what career or direction they could take, but coaching them on goals with priorities for fun, friends and life outside of an office is not often what we focus on.

Who do you want to be? Are you doing that?

What is Purpose? What is My Purpose?

At some point in our life, many of us ask "what our purpose is." Many of us search our entire lifetime, looking outside of ourselves, to find that answer. Our real answer is internal. The answer becomes clear when we focus on *being* versus *doing*. It becomes clear when we let go of those beliefs we have about a title, what we *should* be doing, and what we want to "be when we grow up." Finding purpose equates to finding happiness, and it begins with the I AM. Finding purpose is understanding why we exist.

Once we know the answer to who we are, we can fuel our fire that feeds our CORE.

Self-Assessment

Are you ready to go within and learn what feeds your CORE? The assessment in   Figure 3 will help you determine if you are ready.

Assessment	Yes	No
I just know - I'm ready		
I've been talking for YEARS about making a change		
My friends tell me I need a change		
I have recently gone through a life changing event in my home life such as relocation, divorce, marriage, family addition, care of elderly parent, death		

I have recently gone through change on the job or career such as job transition, new boss, new employees, extended work hours, the push to do more with less		
I am newly entering the work force or thinking of leaving the workforce		
I'm bored, overwhelmed, tired, or not engaged in daily activities and I often wonder if this is all there is		
I dream daily of what I want to be doing		
I spend time thinking of all the things I have to do and never seem to get to them		
I know I need change, I just don't know what to do		
I know what I want, I just don't know how to get there		
I feel like there are never enough hours in the day		
I feel like I do all the work, and others have less responsibility		

Figure 3: Self-Assessment

If you have more than eight items marked "yes," you are ready!

The next step is understanding energy and your CORE energy.

Chapter 2: What Is Energy?

We Are Energy

I am energy, you are energy, and we live in and around varying levels of energy at every moment. The best way I can describe what I see around people or events of energy is this: Think of driving down a long hot stretch of freeway. You see waves of heat on the road that often look like water on the road. These are heat waves of energy. These similar types of energy waves surround us every day, and different events change the depth, impact, color, and range of the waves. They are subtle, yet they are there. What is it and why are we hearing so much about energy? This is not the power or electrical energy that conglomerate organizations produce and sell and that consumers pay for and use. This is the energy that is generated by the planet, the universe, and us. This is our personal energy.

We all vibrate at a certain level, much like the buzzing we hear when we walk underneath power lines. Our vibrations change during the day based on events, the food we eat, and those around us. They change over our lifetimes as we age, move through events such as having children, work stress, the logistics of home life, and many other factors. Everything we do (or do not do) has an energy component, and how we respond (or do not respond to it) impacts our personal energy.

When I walk into rooms and homes, I feel the energy. I look at people and can see their energy. I can also often feel their energy. Many people are in tune with those subtle waves of energy, but more people are not aware of the varying types and waves of energy. They just feel that something is off or different.

If you have ever been to a sporting event where the crowd is excited or upset, you can feel that energy. While living in Minnesota, I spent many years in Minneapolis and went to sporting events at indoor arenas. The

Emerging Energy

Minneapolis dome was known for its noise levels. During a playoff game or World Series events, people often wore ear plugs to prevent damage to their ears. The environment contained energy, but it was more than noise; it was a physical pressure that I could feel on my skin and pushing on my body. The noise of the crowd screaming came after the physical sensation.

Perhaps you have walked into the middle of a fight or disagreement or entered a room where two people argued. A residual energy is often left behind in those situations, and in many cases, that energy does not feel as positively charged as a winning team's energy at a sporting event.

Children's birthday parties are another great example of highly charged energy. Children have limitless energy that they bring to an event when playing and fun are involved.

In the world of healers and intuitive readers, we depend on energy at varying levels. *Reiki*, is a healing energy that pulls energy from source and applies that energy to areas within the body to heal. *Deeksha* is also growing in both knowledge and use, as a way to awaken us to this energy.

Energy is always replenishing itself. It is a circular event; we expend energy, and we pull in energy. Earth healers are pulling in energy to help Mother Earth heal. We work to remove old, stagnant energy from our se so it may be used once again.

To release and pull in energy, we work with the chakra system to ensure that energy flows through the body. "Chakra" is a Sanskrit word that means "wheel". We have our physical body, but we also have a subtle body that consists of channels of energy. Where two or more channels of energy cross in the body, a chakra exists. Chakras are energy centers and are the easiest place to exchange energy with the outside world. If a chakra is blocked, energy remains stuck in that spot. It is like a plugged sink—no more energy can enter, and the old energy becomes stagnant and smelly.

Many tools can be used to feel and move energy. Tuning forks, Tibetan bowls, or Tibetan chimes, water, music, and many more. In understanding the components of energy and the tools to work with energy, we can better use them as positive instruments.

Why Is My Energy Important?

I use my energy to function. From a minimalist's point of view, my energy gets me up in the morning and keeps me moving. It is what I awake to each day, how I feel, and the core of how I am. Everything on this planet has a vibration level, and my energy is how I am vibrating each day. It is how I feel.

I am sensitive to energy, and I can quickly assess an individuals energy level. If vibrations are at an extremely high speed, this may translate to edginess, fidgeting, anxiety, stress, nervousness, all terms we are familiar with. If vibrations are at a lower speed an individual may feel sluggish, depressed, disengaged, and feel like going back to bed.

When I am aware of energy and my energy levels, I can manipulate them or find ways to balance the energy. I often see people attempt to balance energy with food or beverages. Caffeine in the morning may be a way to wake up and get energy. Sugar is another way, and some people start their day with coffee or soda pop and a donut or sugar-coated cereal. These are temporary replenishments for our energy system, but they are not sustainable. When the food or beverage wears off, our energy systems crash, and we look for a refuel option. These are often quick-fix snacks.

We need food for sustenance to the body, and balanced nutrition is important, but sometimes even with good nutrition, we need other forms of energy. This energy can be pulled from the earth or the sky. This is Mother Earth energy or the divine energy, and it is available to us at all times.

When I am without this energy, no amount of food on this planet will sustain me. This is the energy that fills my mind and my spirit and pushes and pulls me to live. This is the energy that fills my soul and thus fills me. This energy is free and unlimited!

To get up and do what I do every day, it is important to know my energy levels, what impacts them, and how to replenish them.

How We Give Away Energy

When I meet people, I feel their energy levels, I see their energy aura, and I look for holes or blockages in their aura or energy flow.

If our energy is flowing and we are full, like a glass filled to the top, we have a brightness or glow about our aura. We feel good and have excitement or enjoyment about life in general.

When I feel the energy, I check in on how I am feeling with my own energy. If I was feeling good and now I am feeling low energy, I know the person's energy is low. If I feel edgy, their energy is ramped up, and they are vibrating at a higher level than I am. I then see their aura and look for a general flow of energy around and through them. Sometimes I see sparks flying from an individual if his energy is charged and flowing and he is ramped up. Sometimes this energy flow is bright white or another bright color, and sometimes it appears muted or dull. If the energy is flowing, I can see this and for the person, this usually mirrors his level of excitement or optimism. He may appear chatty and engaged in the interaction. This does not mean he *must* be talking, but he does appear to be interested. He may be nervous, and this would also show sparks or bright light.

If I am not able to see his energy field or it is muted and even sometime blotchy, it usually means there are holes in his aura. Often I can see the holes or can see the energy pouring from these holes and the energy seeping away.

Holes are usually created when we give away our energy or when someone or a situation we are in is pulling our energy. A person does not have to be physically near us to be pulling our energy, and we do not have to be physically in a situation to have a memory, or an old event, continue to pull energy from us. A relationship break that has not completely healed will continue to pull on our energy. A lingering illness or lingering concern about people or situations will continue to create leaks in our aura.

The individual may speak in terms of a drain on energy or how she is so tired of the situation. These are energy leaks.

Many of us have learned to replenish our energy stores, but we continue to give away energy, sometimes knowingly and sometime unknowingly. The best way to explain this is the feeling you may have after being around someone who drains your energy. You feel fine when you are with him, but in his presence or after he leaves, you feel drained or depleted. He has just filled up on your energy and is bouncing happily along, leaving you empty. He has created a hole in your aura and pulled energy out through that hole.

We also may have holes left by situations or emotions we have not dealt with. They create a slow drip of energy but sometimes not enough to notice until after some time has passed. Sometimes, many years can go by with this slow drip. We learn to operate with minimal energy or we have found small ways to replenish, yet we are not running at the optimal levels.

This is giving away your energy. When you feel depleted, pay attention to what you have just experienced or what you are in the middle of and understand that something in your life is pulling your energy.

I often see blocked energy. This means that the energy has stopped flowing and is stuck in one spot. This energy builds up and becomes stale. Without a clear flow of energy, other parts of our aura are starved of energy, and the blocked areas are stuck with stale energy. We often describe ourselves as "stuck in a rut" or unable to move past a situation. We maintain "sameness" but are unable to move forward or move on.

How to Keep Our Energy

One way to keep our energy is to plug the holes. Remove the things in our lives that put the holes there or that create the slow leaks and the draining feeling. That is easier said than done. Many, if not all, of us at one time or many times in our lives have situations that we cannot move from for a period of time. For example, taking care of ailing parents or becoming a caregiver in a relationship can become a drain. We cannot walk away, but if we do not learn tools and practices to maintain our own energy levels, the situation becomes unsustainable. Many individuals that do not learn to protect and replenish their energy stores become sick themselves. They burn out, and as time goes on without a longer-term solution, replenishment becomes more difficult. I often see people turn to other activities to numb their lives so they no longer feel the drain. Overeating, alcoholism, drugs, or avoiding close relationships and commitments are indicators that energy is void and the person is unable to recharge and replenish.

To have healthy energy, we can use exercises and tools to remove the energy that drains us and plug the holes. Other practices help pull in fresh energy and keep the flow moving so that you can give pure energy to others while maintaining your own energy field.

When people are angry with you or say negative things about you, they attack your aura. They attach negative energy, or cords, to your aura. When they see that they can pull from your energy to sustain their energy, they also attach cords to your energy aura. In your aura, this looks like a cobweb that is wrapped over you. The cords can appear white, gray or black, depending on the length of time they have been attached to you, the depth of energy they are pulling, and the situation they are pulling from. Outright hatred and deep anger for someone would be a black cord; a comment about what they are wearing or other judgment may appear as a white cord. A repeated judgment, over time, appears thinner and may turn gray and then black. My son often asks for help to clear his aura after shopping trips that include angry customers trying to get through a busy store. We may pick up cords from people who are frustrated in general and are throwing angry cords to any one in sight. This would look like a "super soaker water gun" that hits about anyone in its path as it sprays, even innocent bystanders.

Exercise

Remove any cords or negative energy you are holding in your aura or that have been thrown on your aura. The methods to do this are described below.

1. **Wipe off negative energy** that is clinging to you by wiping off your arms: run your hands down the length of your arms from shoulders to wrists. Wipe both arms from the center of your body, and in the heart area, cup your hands and push the energy from your center (heart) down to the earth. This takes negative energy and pushes it to Mother Earth for healing and rejuvenation. Do not worry about contaminating Mother Earth. This is her way of healing the energy and reusing it for the betterment of all. There was a time that I felt I was polluting her with negative energy from clients as I pulled contaminated energy from, and she calmed that concern. She welcomes this healing as a way for all of us to live more cleanly in our environments.

2. **Visualize cutting cords** by thinking of a big scissors cutting the cords that are attached to you. Kids love this one, as they can pretend that their first two fingers are doing all the cutting. Some of my dear friends like visualizing gathering those cords around them, pulling them above their head, and then cutting them with one, big arm swoop above their head. Others imagine pulling them off their bodies and throwing them to Mother Earth for healing. All these methods create a visual of removing the cords and negative energy from your body or aura and sending them off for healing.

Once you have removed the old cords and no longer have any attachment (from the external sources pulling your energy), you can protect yourself from reattachments. The easiest way to do this is to surround yourself in pure, white, divine energy. Envision a white light showering down over your entire body, like a shower would cover you in water. Another method is to think of this white light encasing your body like a mummy wrapped in gauze. The white light is a protective layer that blocks future cords from becoming attached. It acts like as a shield, and the cords will not stick or embed themselves in your aura.

These are easy ways to block energy depletions from external sources, but what about internal sources of giving our energy away? These can be situations or lifestyles that we hold onto that continue to contaminate our environment. Recognizing what these situations are is the first step to letting them go. Once we recognize them and the impact they have on us, we can chose to continue or to let them go.

If we keep them, we must have methods to replenish our stores. It is unrealistic to believe that we can live without ever being in situations that drain us. It is much more important to learn to use the tools to replenish our energy stores so that we have the energy to address any longer-term drains.

How to Restore Energy

We may take many actions to restore our energy or to keep ourselves running, and we may try many different methods, or variations of those methods, as a way to refuel. Some of our methods are temporary and may only avoid dealing with the root issue. Some might be short term and we accept that, and others are more sustainable. Knowing and finding how we refuel is important, and this requires us to pay attention and identify when we feel filled up and when we feel depleted. When we feel depleted, it means making a conscience effort to refuel versus using a temporary method to avoid knowing that we are energy drained. Shopping, gaming activities, sporting events, eating, drinking, working crazy hours, or working multiple jobs are methods to fill our time with, and they may be temporary activities. These are also examples of doing activities versus being activities. These activities feel good for a short time, but we may feel remorse later. We have not really refueled but got a short-term adrenaline fix. These are not sustainable activities, and they are outward versus internal, thereby creating a residual cost.

This describes how I was when I went on that vacation to Sedona with my family. It was a "doing" vacation, and the energy from running and doing kept me running at a high level, but it was not sustainable. For my family, a "doing" vacation was depleting, and they wanted to relax and enjoy quiet time.

Exercising, regular outings with friends, or other planned activities that refill and sustain us may be healthier from a long-term standpoint, but they still depend on "doing."

It is easy to replenish energy reserves by drawing from sources or from the divine by focusing on "being" and breathing energy into our bodies. Yoga and other meditation forms are wonderful for helping us get centered and replenish our energy stores. Once we are full, we are much more able to give clean energy without feeling drained. This creates a balance in energy. It is not "give or take" but "give and receive."

Usable Energy and Reserve Energy
Not all energy is usable. When we have pure energy and a steady flow of energy, we are more able to give usable energy, which can be sent to others for help or healing. To use healing energy requires a fluid flow, and it is important that anyone who does healing work understands and stays in a clear flow of energy. When we have gray, black, or shadowed energy, we do not want to share this energy. Novice healers may send this energy without understanding what they are doing and the impact on those they are working with.

When we have pure energy, we are in a state of bliss and joy, and energy emanates from within. All we think about is giving love and joy to those around us. This is the state mature healers work in when they are working with others. They do not see clients when they are not able to maintain this level of energy. I had a mentor who canceled appointments with her clients. They often did not understand and saw her as inconsistent or unorganized rather than understanding that it was related to her need to remain pristine. In the end, she stopped seeing clients for fear of upsetting them and that in itself created a drain on her.

Before we can give energy to anyone, we must fill our internal stores and maintain a level of purity. I have done full-day workshops where I see ten to fifteen clients. I may not do not stop to eat and have found that if I do not think about it, I do not drink much water either. People ask if I am tired, believing that the energy pull to do so many readings or healing is a pull on me. The energy is not pulled from me at all. In fact, I am pulling in pure energy throughout the day; it refills me, and I send this pure energy to my clients. It is a continuous flow of energy that has only one place to go—to the client.

Bad Energy

I have been asked many times about bad energy or dark energy and if I ever feel this. I work with the divine and pure energy and do not allow other energies to "tag onto me" or anyone I work with. I do not allow it. If we never allow dark energy to be part of our aura, we do not need to be concerned about it. If you are faced with a situation where dark energy is involved, protect yourself. The closest I have been to dark energy is the few times I have been asked to clear a home where the owner said there was an energy that did not feel good, or when I have walked into the middle of a awful argument. Some reality TV shows are examples of bad energy or dark energy that, if we allow it, can cling to us.

Clearing bad energy in a home, room, or office can be done by imagining a large fan blowing the dark energy outside or filling the room with light-white energy. You may also burn sage in a room and let the smoke clear residual energy.

Barriers that Prevent Clear Energy Flow

We create our own barriers, and when we do, we are not able to release the energy that is associated with an event. Fear of letting go of a situation or relationship that no longer serves us often feels safer than the unknown. We may have become so numb or accustomed to an aura with holes in it that we do not know what an energized aura feels like. We may feel we do not deserve to be filled, do not believe in energy, or do not understand it, and we dismiss the opportunity to learn what might be available for us.

When people do not understand energy, I ask them if they have ever attended a sporting event where the crowds where wild. Could they feel the energy? I ask if they have ever been in an argument or walked into a room where an argument just took place and could "almost cut the air in the room with a knife." If you have ever felt completely drained when being with someone, or found yourself in a career or situation that pulls energy from you, you will want to understand energy and how to refuel it.

Measuring Your Energy Level

How do you know you are functioning at your maximum potential for energy, or have you become numb and it is time to wake up?

There may be times when we begin to refuel and wake up and it is an odd feeling, so we stop. We may be in families or careers that once we refuel, we also feel odd, which may make us stop.

On April 10, 2011, *The Wall Street Journal Europe* posted a special report on energy. The article "Earth savings: How to reduce energy consumption, save money and help the environment" was written by Javier Espinoza.

In his well-written article, he explains what consumers and companies can do to save energy and money. He highlights that can also be applied to those areas beyond our physical environments. The same principles apply to how we use and conserve energy within our bodies.

"**Put that light out**

Conventional lighting is one of the key areas homeowners should tackle to reduce their electricity bills. In the U.K. people spend about GBP 2.4 billion on electricity to power their lighting.

This represents a whopping 17% of all of the world's energy and electricity consumption in buildings. "If consumers buy compact fluorescent lamps, or CFLs, they can make a significant difference in their energy consumption," says the IEA's Mr. Bradley. "Incandescent bulbs will last about 1,000 hours but a CFL lasts 5,000 hours."[1]

Like our use of electricity, we can conserve our own energy. We can "put the lights out, dim the lights," and focus energy usage where required and needed.

When we spend time on self-talk, going over all the things we should have done but didn't, we expend energy. When we spend time churning through situations and play out all the good, bad, and ugly that might occur prior to any event even happening, we expend energy. We burn energy when we often do not really need to. Mind chatter is often when we beat ourselves up, and that's not productive. When we move through a situation without mind chatter, we reserve that energy for purposeful thoughts that move us forward.

On one of my international trips, I panicked when I was told there would be free time and we would have an opportunity to go scuba diving in a pristine beach area of Brazil. I feared both my business acquaintances seeing me in a swimsuit and the fact that I'd never gone scuba diving.

I could not decide which fear was worse. I could imagined not going on the trip, purposely forgetting my swimsuit, protective beach cover-up attire, and on and on and on. My head was swimming! I talked to numerous friends and family about how to approach this problem. I went shopping at least eight times, looking for the perfect beach attire. I spend a fair amount of time at a pool in the summer and have many swimsuits, but I was using all my energy around a non-problem. The problem was all in my head.

Espinoza's article recommendation to "check for cavities":

> "Most homes are under-insulated so increasing insulation is a very easy way to be cost effective. Moving to more efficient windows will make a lot of difference, according to the IEA. The Energy Saving Trust estimates homeowners could potentially save GBP 160 on annual heating bills by identifying "cavities" or heat lost in a property as a result of poor insulation. But buyer beware. A recent investigation by consumer affairs organization which found that mis-selling and bad advice is rife."[i]

Just as we insulate our homes, we often attempt to insulate ourselves. We may numb our senses with drugs, alcohol, or food. We may carry extra weight that prohibits others from getting close to us. Many of us are not aware of how our bodies feel. We have become accustomed to a certain energy level that becomes normal level. It is not until we shift the energy that we can truly understand how we were feeling.

Many of us create energy leaks without even knowing or understanding that we have done so. An energy leak is like a hole in our aura which often leaves us feeling empty or drained. An energy leak is like a leak in an tire. It can be a slow leak or a big hole. You can continue to drive on the tire as long as you continue to refill the tire. You can drive this way for a while if you choose, but if not repaired, it will become a flat tire. A hole in your aura can also drain energy from your field and leave you feeling flat.

To sustain our energy for purposeful use, we must block energy leaks and then replenish with practices such as healthy food, water, exercise, minimizing stress, restful sleep, and playtime.

Another relevant point in Espinoza's article is to "better your batteries":

> "Despite advances in other energy saving technology, batteries remain bulky and don't last long enough. This could be about to change. IBM is working on a battery that could potentially last 10 times longer than the average battery in use today. "Batteries may disappear altogether in smaller devices," says Lucy Chapman of IBM U.K. "By rethinking the basic building block of electronic devices, the transistor, IBM is aiming to reduce the amount of energy per transistor to less than 0.5 volts. With energy demands this low, we might be able to lose the battery altogether in some devices like mobile phones or e-readers."i

Our energy is our battery. Our energy runs us, and without it, we run slow or don't run at all. Better batteries include the fuels that recharge us. It is time to wake up your sensors and know what your potential is. It is time to rate your energy and what you can build to.

Rate Your Energy

Exercise

Six Questions to Rate Energy

Please answer the following	never	2x week	3x week	5x week	7x week	multiple x each day
I find myself smiling for no apparent reason						
I say yes to activities because they will be fun and I WANT to do them						
I have a regular schedule for meals, sleep and exercise						
I look forward to being with people						
I wake ready for a new day						
I look forward to my day						
total						

Scoring

Add each column and multiply the total by the following point value below.

never	-5
2 times per week	1
3 times per week	2
5 times per week	3
7 times per week	4
multiple times each day	5

Analysis

If you have a negative number, you are depleting your energy by these actions and have to work harder to refuel and sustain yourself at a balanced energy level.

Chapter 3: Awakening Within

You never need to ask; you already have. It is all inside, and it is already yours. Stop asking, and claim it. As you claim that which is already yours, remember that life is not an event, it is a journey. You create this journey; you create the event and the outcomes, and therefore, you create your life.

Life is not an event, it is a journey, but many people live their lives based on a series of events versus the experience or the journey. They spend entire lives asleep, numb to what is happening around them or within themselves. They live as a "walking head," entirely unaware of their body or how they feel. People experience events that highlight or guide them along their journey. Typical life events may be learning to ride a bike, driving, graduation, college, a first job, marriage, first car, or first house. Life-changing events may be an accident, divorce, death, loss of job, children, or grandchildren.

To embark upon any journey, most people follow a roadmap. However, in our lives, we often neglect to map our life journey, and we wander our entire lives. What if I had done that? What if I had taken that job, married that person, or went to school for that? We often retrace or take detours to what we want from life rather than setting a map and following it. We do not establish landmark or goal stops along the way, so we never know if we have completed our journey or will meander forever.

These people live their journey based on a vocabulary of *should of, would of,* and *could of.* Some may spend their lives dreaming for the future or never healing from the past. In my years of coaching individuals, managing people, doing intuitive readings, or connecting loved ones with those who have died, there have been many conversations that start with, "I wish I had."

Before your next "I wish I had" moment, begin to look within, and know that looking within is also a life journey. You will not wake up one morning and say that you know yourself. That would be a limited view of all that you are, because it is only that moment in time. To awaken within, you stretch your identity of who you thought you were and learning who you really are. Once you have this information, you are able to reengineer and retool yourself. If you believe you are done or have reached your mountain top, rethink this. We are never done. We are here for life-long learning, and when we do not learn, we repeat lessons. Each day is different, and each day provides unique opportunities to learn about ourselves, the people around us, and the situations we face. Each situation provides a new lens or magnifying glass so that we can learn more.

Learning about yourself is also about finding your home in the world. Some may call this a comfort zone. To me, a comfort zone is a padded room with no threats or stimulants for growth. To stretch or learn about yourself, be uncomfortable. Allow a new sensation in your mind or body. Allow yourself time to assess what that feeling is, what caused it, and what you are or are not going to do about it. Being a life-long learner means stretching and acknowledging that you will never know everything about your spirit but can be open to new learning each day.

All things are connected as one, and all have a place that feels home. Find your home.

Being Quiet to Begin BEING
Time Alone
Take a vacation alone. Do not plan daily events. I thought the perfect vacation was filled with events, seeing things, doing things, and it left little time for just being.

Most Minnesotans go north during the summer months. Many of us rent cabins, but many families own cabins. These are get-away locations meant to be restful, relaxing places to rejuvenate. For most of us, it is home away from home, which means you are also taking the non-vacation-home chores with you, such as dishes, laundry, cooking, grocery shopping, and all those activities that you do at home. Now, they are done by a lake! This vacation also requires a focused effort to do be the entertainment planner, referee (for fighting kids), fishing guide, and life guard, in addition to a dozen jobs that get tagged along such as sweeping the sand from the cabin, hanging up wet towels, and cleaning fish. The vacation responsibilities include unpacking the car and putting away items used for the trip, vacuuming the sand from the vehicle, laundry, and the tasks of settling back in such as grocery shopping or cleaning from the refrigerator the items you forgot before you left for vacation. You feel like you need a vacation from the vacation!

I began my journey to change my life and traveled, alone, to Sedona as my rest and rejuvenation place. The first couple of trips to Sedona were hard for me. I arrived in Phoenix and often used the drive to Sedona for conference calls, catching up with employees, work, or touching base with friends and family. I arrived in Sedona, checked into my hotel, and filled my time with hiking, shopping, driving to see an attraction or the scenery, more hiking, and the other items on my "activity list." I stopped back at the hotel for a change of clothes or something I had forgotten. Because I had my laptop with me and could catch up with email and other work activities, I was always busy. I turned on the TV only for noise, and books were left unread on the night stand.

As my alone time continued, I learned to just be and was able to quiet my busy mind. On one particular trip, I had moved beyond doing and was ready to share the experience. I convinced a dear friend of mine to travel with me. We had talked about this trip for over five years, but we could never get our schedules aligned (one of us was traveling for work, busy on a project or busy with kids). We had both been running at a fast pace on the "doing treadmill." Our schedules finally matched, and we were able to carve out a few days to travel to Sedona. Our first days there were spent time adjusting to the time zone change, the climate, the altitude, and attempting to slow down our lives. Moving from corporate clocks with early morning international conference calls and late-night meetings to this vacation required a more focused effort to just relax.

We had planned a day hike to Sedona's Cathedral Rock. This is my favorite hike, and Cathedral Rock is known as the "heart vortex" or the "heart energy spot" in Sedona and it is known to open your heart chakra. I often take amazing orb or energy photos at Cathedral, and this day I wanted to capture the energy I was sensing around my friend. I was also taking pictures so she could enjoy simply being in the energy without having to worry about taking pictures. She also was busy snapping photos on her Blackberry and sending them to a loved one back in Minnesota. Seeing that she was distracted with photos, connections, and incoming text and email messages, I suggested she find a spot to meditate and that I would come back in about an hour. I left my backpack and phone in my backpack near a tree and began my hike. When I returned an hour later, I found her instant messaging and e-mailing. She was still in do-ing mode and admitted she was having a hard time relaxing.

Remove Distractions
The following day, my corporate friend and I joined my spiritual friend, Indiana Griffon, for another hike. Before we began our hike, I put my phone in my vehicle and suggested to my executive friend that she do the same, assuring her that I had my camera. She shot me the look that said, "You have got to be kidding." I insisted that phones and other electronic devices were going to stay in the vehicle that day. Indiana Griffon laughed at our discussion; he may have surmised that this was like asking my friend to remove her right arm. After assuring her that she would be fine, we left for our hike. Removing all distractions created an opening for the new to enter. Distraction detracts from what we are

receiving. Being alone not only means away from people but also the things that keep us in a "busy" state of mind.

We busy our minds and our bodies with so much *doing* that there is no time for discovering who we are or who the people are that we are *being* with. This happens in our home life, family, and career. On the first day back on the job from a vacation, you may find you are ready for a vacation again, and your time off is a vague memory. The reality is that you can only *do* your best when you are your best *being*. Most of us have never taken the journey to discover our *being*.

My first solo visits to Sedona were hard lessons in being and letting go of planning, itineraries, and activities. I discovered that when I did not have something planned, was not doing and could not connect with anyone, I was by myself for periods of time. The universe provided a method for me to *be* with no distractions.

On one trip to Sedona, I complained all week that I was not getting email on my Blackberry. My connection at the hotel was questionable. In the end, I gave up trying to connect, but this did little to calm my need to be connected. My phone seemed to be working fine, but no email was coming through. Being in the technology world and for years supporting servers, email, and systems in general, I went into "troubleshoot mode" and thought it must be an email server issue. I left a phone message for my support team to call if it needed any help with the server issues. I heard nothing from the team members, so I believed they had it under control and went about enjoying my time hiking. On the *last* day of my trip, as I was standing in a location I had stood at a dozen times over the week, my emails began to download. At this same time, I received a call from my office telling me there was never a problem and all was fine on their end. We were thirty minutes away from leaving for the airport, and the universe was telling me it was all right to move back to the work world and allowed distractions once again. Anything prior to this would have taken away from the experience and the messages that I was apparently there to focus on. The logical side of me wanted to reason away what had just happened. Certainly it must be the Blackberry server and not something like energy that was blocking my email, right?

The lesson of the trip was loud and clear: Once you open the door to the universe to allow clear energy to enter without distractions, the universe appears to work toward that goal. On each subsequent visit to Sedona or any other site that I visit, I remain open and not at all surprised when blocks are added or removed. I go with the flow and remember that there is a greater message for me to be aware of.

Plan Time Alone
It is important to refresh, rejuvenate, and re-group your inner being by taking time alone. If you cannot take a vacation; take time out of your day, every day, to be alone. Close and lock the door. I know a woman who hangs a sign on the door of her home office, "Do not enter unless the house is on fire or flooding or if someone is bleeding profusely."

Being from a Midwest family of do-ers that centered on doing and creating a tangible output from that doing, I have always found it difficult to sit, relax, and just be. Just *being* was not doing something. It is funny how we can sit for hours and watch TV, surf the Internet, or play video games and reason that we are being productive. These activities distract us from going within and understanding our inner self. Meditating, journaling, or sitting quietly feels like we are not doing anything, and for many, that is not okay. In all actuality, time that we give to the mind is the most productive of all. It opens and clarifies questions that have been spinning in our heads for years. Many people find it impossible to be quiet for ten minutes.

Other Practices to Find the *Being* within Journaling
Does journaling bring back memories of having a diary when you were young? If someone read your most personal thoughts, the thought of journaling may be fearful. Perhaps you believe that journaling is writing with purpose, and you have convinced yourself that you do not know

how to write, will never write a book, and it is a waste of time. I journal every day, sometimes multiple times a day. I use journaling for getting thoughts down on paper as much as to clear my thoughts and regain focus. I may journal at work if it helps clear my mind or bring enlightenment on a situation.

Journal on paper with pencil or pen. It might be easier or faster with computers, but the connection between mind, eye, and hand is important. Some people use the excuse that they have sloppy handwriting and so they "could never" journal, but handwriting does not matter. Journaling is often done without an expected outcome, meaning it will not turn into a book or story (unless it is adapted or developed for that specific purpose). This type of journaling is to simply get thoughts on paper and clear your mind. The thoughts do not need to be linear or complete.

When I travel by air, I always take a notebook or my journal. After one particular busy flight, I found myself with reams of handwritten notes. I took a few days to reread, sort, and keep or toss material. I was amazed at the thoughts that had poured from my mind. There were both actions plans and junk that my mind was holding on to, like a garbage can for the mind.

It is like cleaning your closet every year. Organizers who focus on helping people with home storage, particularly closets, advise people that if you have not worn something in two years, toss or donate it. Cleaning out a closet allows you to fit more stuff in it or find what you already have. If you think of your mind as a big closet, journaling is like clearing or cleaning space. You can toss what is not needed or find and organize what you did not know you had. By clearing and organizing your mind, you allow space for new thoughts, ideas, and information. When our minds become cluttered, we get stuck and do not move beyond the clutter to discover new information. How can you possibly allow anything new to enter when you are walking over all the old junk? Just like closets, some of our thoughts, beliefs, or actions may be left over from another era. No one likes outdated clothes in their closet, and the same applies to your mental closet.

After losing a weight, I cleaned out my closet and found my favorite business suit, which was a "measuring stick" for me. If I could fit back into that suit, I would know that my body was back to the shape I had before kids, before stress, and before years of not focusing on exercising. I pulled the suit from its dust bag and tried it on. It was baggy on me, but I would not wear it even if it did fit. Remember the football-sized shoulder pads of the 1980s? The shoulder pads and the plaid print were no longer my style, and they certainly were not the style of the current corporate environment. After I wiped away tears of laughter, I sat for a moment. WOW!! How many years did I hold onto that suit, telling myself that *someday* I would wear it again? That "someday" had come and gone.

How many things do we hold in our minds that we think we will come back to someday? When the someday comes, the world has changed, and so have we.

Clear your mind, and purge what does not fit or does not work anymore. Do not hold onto what worked once. Even when an idea may fit again, the style is probably not right anymore. When you journal, dump it on paper.

Journaling Practice
Set a timer for ten minutes, and write. It does not have to be a story, and it can be about something or nothing. Write whatever comes to mind. Watch your paper fill with words and thoughts. The words and thoughts do not need to make sense. Sometimes we believe that everything we write must be a well-formulated thought, sentence and idea. Just write. If you would like, when you are done, set it aside to read later or toss.

Meditate

STOP   The word "meditate" may make you shutter. You might feel like skipping this section, or you might already have thought, "I can't." Does it feel like I have asked you to commit a crime? Please read on!!!

It seems that all my friends have tried meditation. They either love it or hate it. Those who hate it give up and never try again. They tell me, "I tried it, and I just can't do it, so don't even ask." Why try *anything* if you have made up your mind that you cannot do it or you are going to fail again? Perhaps you have never tried to meditate, but after listening to friends claim they are not able, you believe that you will not even try. Perhaps you believe that it is hard or there is a *perfect* way to meditate.

Start with no expectation about what the experience will be and whether you fail or succeed. There is no test. The beauty of this practice is that it becomes whatever you want it to be. The secret is to start small. The purpose is to relax and quiet your mind, and if you are stressed about something that is meant to relax you, change your thoughts about it. If during meditation your mind runs wild, let it run wild, and see what happens.

I used to meet my brother regularly for coffee. Talk about a do-er and busy-minded guy! His biggest complaint was that he was not able to shut off his mind, was not able to relax, and just be. Growing up with him, I found that I could never go with him to visit someone. Just as I was settling in, he would be ready to get up and go and was always onto the next thing. He was never present with the people he was with. My parents complained that he could not sit still, and in many ways, we were similar growing up: both busy and always on the go. One coffee one morning, he commented that not only had my physical body changed, but I emanated a youthful and relaxed presence. He asked how I had learned to relax. I suggested that he meditate, and his reaction was "no way." He was too busy, and his mind would never allow him to do that. He spent five minutes telling me all the reasons that he could not meditate. I could feel how his energy had elevated due to stress.

Many people believe that when they mediate, they will instantly know how and what to do. When I first meditated, I could be still for a few minutes at a time. Thoughts and the pressure to get up and go do something always came crashing in, and I got up to go do something. I did that many times before I dealt with the guilt of sitting and doing nothing. Clearing your mind takes work, and it does not come naturally for everyone. The brain works naturally and is continually energized. Your neurons are always firing, even when you have quiet time, so to think that you can shut it off right away is unrealistic.

When I started meditating, I needed to let go of what I thought it was supposed to be. There have been many times that I allowed my mind to wander and let any and all thoughts enter. There is not a right or wrong way to meditate; the purpose is releasing the clutter.

Exercise
Easy Meditation Starter Practice
Set a timer for five minutes. During this time, sit or lie down, and close your eyes. Float, see what happens when you clear your thoughts, or let your thoughts run away. Letting your thoughts run away may be clearing them from your brain space. Much like a computer has temporary storage that needs to be cleared for reuse, your brain may contain temporary thoughts that need to be cleared.

Exercise Your Mind
It is as important to exercise your mind as it is to exercise your body. When you exercise your mind, do so with quality in mind. Avoid regularly reading magazines filled with stories about the drama in other people's lives and avoid gossip. Focus on your own life and not the drama of others. By focusing outside yourself, you avoid your own life; stay clear in your own mind and focus there. Choose reading material that is meaningful, without drama, and that provides clear messages. . When you nourish your body, you think of healthy food. Think of nourishing your mind with healthy information.

For years, I convinced myself that after a busy day, I deserved to lounge on the couch the entire night. I worked hard all day, so didn't I have that right to just sit and do nothing in the evening? If you think about it, I was doing something: putting mush into my brain; watching TV all night, reading gossip magazines, and playing solitaire on the computer.

These mindless activities were my attempts to forget my day and relax, but I never felt rejuvenated. Often, I stayed up late and woke up tired. Rejuvenate your mind and body by reading healthy books or healthy information. Shut off the TV.

Exercise
Easy Brain Starter Practice

Choose a book of daily affirmations. It does not have to be written specifically for this purpose but can be any self-help book in the area you want to focus on. If you want to get organized, choose a book around organization. If you want to find your purpose in life, pick up a book on finding purpose. Visit a book store and walk though the self-help isles and choose a book that is calling to you. You do not have to read the book from cover to cover, but open it to, each day, to any page, and read a paragraph that jumps out to you. You would be surprised at how the messages align to where you are that day and help you to focus.

Exercise
Exercise Your Body

Shut off the TV. Spend time exercising your body and nourishing your mind. Just as you eat to nourish your physical being, nourish your cells by exercising. When you exercise, breathing elevates as blood pumps and delivers oxygenated blood. This means great energy for your body.

During my visits to Sedona, I got up early, showered, had a quick, healthy breakfast, and went hiking. I took my journal, pen, book, and water. As I began my walks, I was locked into thoughts of career, home, kids and other issues. The longer I walked, the more I noticed those thoughts giving way, and I began to notice the trees, plants, and birds. Nature gives us an opportunity to enjoy her if we pay attention to the plants and animals around us. What lessons is life giving you?

It is hard to go outside in Minnesota in the winter. It may be impossible during periods of subzero temperatures, but there are many places you can go to move. Even moving indoors is better than not moving at all. You can walk at a mall, join a health club, or run up and down stairs. Even walking or moving multiple times per day is better than not moving at all. Pay attention, track how much you are moving, and be purposeful with practices that require more movement.

Many people habitually take shallow breaths, and when you exercise, you take deeper breaths, which elevates energy. Taking deeper breaths brings more oxygen into the blood and clears the brain. Clearing your brain allows more clear thoughts, ideas, and dreams to enter your brain space.

When we quiet ourselves, we can listen to messages of spirit or of the earth. To hear those messages, we must first quiet ourselves. When we do so, the awakening within can begin.

Chapter 4: Listening and Hearing

Listening

There are particular spots where I love to sit quietly and listen to nature: birds singing or chirping, frogs, crickets, cicadas, the scurrying of lizards and bugs as they rustle through the dirt or leaves, the wind. These are sounds that we hear and recognize. What about the sounds we have tuned out? What messages can we gain from these sounds? Listening to nature is listening to *all* of nature, including trees, plants, rocks, and other aspects we have not been taught to listen to and therefore we have tuned them out.

When I meditate in my favorite spots, I am able listen to nature. Many spots have been found unintentionally, but once realized, they have become favorite spots. One such spot is in Sedona at the airport vortex. Vortexes are high energy spots on the Earth. This particular energy spot is known for its drive for results or a place to put ideas, and intents forth to the universe for forward action. From this spot, you can see other well known vortexes and energy spots such as Cathedral, Bell Rock, Court House and many other Sedona landmarks. More important, you can feel the energies and hear many things if you quiet your mind and listen with openness.

At this site, I have found a tree that I sit near. The first time that I sat by this tree, it was nearing 100 degrees. The only reason I sat down was to drink some water and cool off, but the stillness of the area pulled me in. I pulled my journal from my backpack and settled in, ready to write. I had just flown in from Minneapolis, and after a busy week, I wanted to use the time to clear my head and focus on where my next few weeks would be spent. I had my corporate job on my mind, and though I was sitting on a rock in Sedona, it was "strategizing time" for me. Before I could get my first word down on paper, I began to hear the tree creak. The dryness of the heat and air created a language for the tree. I turned to him and smiled; now that he had gotten my attention, I was able to focus on him and listen. (I identified him as a male energy.) I believe that rocks, tress, and plants speak to us. If you listen closely, you can hear nature speaking to you and you can feel the buzz of energy. When I sat quietly and listened to the trees, I heard the messages from nature. Some of my most inspirational messages and clarity on my life came to me by that tree. Some of my questions, long unanswered, were answered, and some of my most productive days have included sitting out in nature. I was inspired, motivated, and deeply energized.

Messages for us are everywhere. Chatter and conversations and answers are available to us, and silence allows for quiet and inward thoughts.

Paying Attention

In my corporate job, I work with global team members who have rules for the etiquette of meetings and conference calls: beware of time zones, do not multitask, repeat a question before answering, identify yourself, do not assume that people will know your voice, and so on. They center on being focused and paying attention. These are simple rules, and many people wonder why they are needed, but speaking with an unfocused audience is frustrating.

When I was around eight or nine years old, I wrote to my uncle. He working in Chicago as a priest, and my mother encouraged me to write to him to practice my penmanship. On one occasion, I asked about talking to the angels and the messages they shared with me. He said that yes, I can talk to the angels and God anytime. I wrote again, asking more specifically about hearing angels. He again said that I could talk to God, go to church, and listen to my parents. He never addressed my questions about hearing angels, and I stopped writing to him after that. I am sure angels continued to speak to me, but I stopped paying attention to their messages. I tuned them out.

I learned a lesson about the importance of listening and paying attention to messages, even the message embedded within a child's question. With my own children, I am positive there have been and will be times where I do not hear their message or the real question, but I believe that focus on the conversation at hand is critical. When I do intuitive readings, I often ask the angels for clarity or to repeat their message so to ensure I have heard or interpreted their message clearly. I always pause and ask them if there is more in their message. In other words, would they like to say anything else. Paying attention to subtle messages and any feelings I get when working with people is important. To do so, I must shut off all distractions and focus. If I am on the phone I look at the phone as if I am face to face with that person, or I close my eyes and envision the person in my mind's eye.

These lessons on paying attention and focusing are important for you and for everyone that you interact with.

Removing Your Blinders
A friend and I discussed meditation and how walking can be a way of meditating. She preferred walking in the woods and asked me about the hiking I'd done in Sedona. I grew up in Minnesota, spent summers fishing Minnesota lakes, and have many favorite hiking spots. There are many magical hiking places around the world, and Sedona has known energy vortexes, but there are also many unknown energy spots. I told her about some of the photos I had taken on a few of the trails where I had captured pixies, angels, and orbs in the photos. I gravitated to some favorite trails as if all the trees were calling to me, waiting to have someone new to talk to and someone that would listen to them. I have favorite meditation spots where the energy seems to swirl around and then drop right into me and other places where it feels like energy is pushing up from Mother Earth through me to reach the sky. I watched my friend's eyes widen. She asked if I would think she was crazy if she told me that she found that some trees had such energy that she needed to reach out and touch them as she walked by them, as if they were a dear friend and she needed to give them a loving pat. She waited for my response.

I told her I did not think that was crazy at all. I touch rocks, plants and trees all the time. I talk to and touch trees and have even given many trees full-body hugs. Some trees make me smile, and many times I wait for them to respond through their messages, a fallen leaf, or a gentle rustling of leaves. I have found trees that appear to have facial expressions and looking at them makes me smile or laugh. I have walked through a forest of oak trees and have had them drop acorns on me as a way to get me to pay attention and communicate with them. I asked her if that sounded crazy!

We laughed at how rigid life can be, with rules around nature and what you do or don't hear. Who made up these silly rules? If you have ever gone parasailing or hang gliding, you will experience silence like never before. There are no sounds but the wind. When you open your mind, remove the rules, and take off the blinders you have given yourself, you see in a new way. This is creating a new lens for you.

Seeing with a New Lens
I sat at Cathedral Rock, another favorite spot in Sedona. It was early morning, and it was going to be a hot day. I went for a hike near the river, determined to take my new-found knowledge of hearing nature and nature's messages to a new level. I asked to be guided for more information. I stopped at a point along the trail where the river changes direction, and it was a perfect spot to sit, eat my breakfast, and write down some thoughts. Perhaps I could get some help from nature. I was troubled by some decisions I had made in my life. As I studied the river running toward me, I thought about the similarities in how the river was running to how I was feeling about my life.

I sat down on the edge of the rocks and took my shoes off. The water was cool in contrast to the heat of the rocks. My head pounded, and I wondered why I had gotten up so early. Still distracted by the chatter in my head (or maybe it was the pounding), I snapped a few photos. It had been an interesting week in the office, and I had much work ahead of me, getting my teams aligned. I had struggles at home with the kids focusing on their school work and how their grades would impact their college choices. I was contemplating a move from Minnesota that would mean uprooting the kids from family, friends and schools. I wondered if this would be a good decision; was the timing off for any decision? Perhaps the best decision was no decision at all? I desperately wanted to know the right answer and choose what would be best for all of us. My head was swimming with what-if scenarios.

I looked upstream at Cathedral Rock, still feeling a heaviness in my heart. I could feel the energy from this area move through my body and I began to focus on clearing thoughts from my head. We learn early to think through a situation, define the options, list the pros and cons, and make a decision. I had further learned this structured approach to planning by leading projects and teams through situations that required writing the options on a white board. *Discuss, decide, champion* entered my head. To clear my head without making a decision would be *procrastination* or *avoidance*. I heard, loud and clear, a voice that told me to clear my head and listen.

I looked around to see where the voice had come from. I studied the trees and waited for them to talk, but there was nothing, no one. They refused to help solve my dilemma. Something shimmered in the water, and I focused my eyes there. I heard it again. *Clear your head and listen.* I watched the water flow downstream and swirl around. As the water approached a rock, some water went to the right of the rock and some to the left. How did the water know which side to go and what to follow? My mind began to wander, and my thoughts became a study of the water. What if it was a family of drops, and they got separated in the stream? When they came to the divide in the river, how did they know which way to go? One divide took them downstream, but the other dumped into a holding area. What about the drops of water that ended up on top of the rocks, soon to be evaporated by the hot sun, taken to the clouds to join other drops? "Oh good grief," I thought, "thinking about water-drop-families and their journeys is crazy—but then again, not so crazy."

We have many routes in our lives, and none are guaranteed. Some decisions take us on routes that follow a continuous path, while others follow the same route and deviate along the way. Some of us end up on the rocks and are recycled at a later time. All of us "droplets" have purpose, such as sustaining plants, fish or water-life, while for some of us, our purpose is to carry others downstream. Some of us join together and create something new, like a new path or stream. "Wow, we are human rivers," I thought. I marveled at the lesson this river gave me as each drop pushed onward, as if it had intent and purpose. Did it? Did it know its purpose, or was it "going with the flow"?

I began to listen. Why was it so important that I know all my moves and actions when many of the areas in my life were beyond my control? I needed to relax and go with the flow. I needed to understand that whatever journey I decided to take, it would be fine, and in the end, I would do what I was meant to do. Just go.

I left Cathedral Rock refreshed and more confident than I had been in weeks. Nature provided me insight into how I was feeling and the fears that were rising within me. To put words to what I was experiencing, I needed to quiet my mind, be still, and allow my mind to be curious. My mind was not without thought. Most people believe that "quieting the mind" is to empty it from thought. For me, relaxing and letting my mind be clear, turning forced thoughts to wandering thoughts, allowed me to find the answers I was looking for.

New Lens

What does having a new lens mean? Why do I want to look through it, and why is that so important? In my early twenties, I was told that I look at life "through rose-colored glasses." I spent some time thinking about the saying; obviously, it had to do with looking at life through pink glasses, but it also meant I looked at life with optimism, maybe missing a few flaws in life by overlooking them. I did not know why that was such a bad thing. I discussed this with some of my friends. Wasn't it a good thing that I was optimistic in how I looked at life? We believed that was better to look at life with optimism versus being hesitant or pessimistic. We wanted to be bold and believe this. I believed that even if my "glasses" were rose colored, I could take them off or put them on at any time. I interpreted the saying in my own way.

I remain extremely optimistic; however, I am older now and somewhat wiser. I have had the opportunity to live through many situations in life, home, career, and kids, and I know that at times I kept those glasses on too long. There may have been times that I hoped for something that was never going to happen. Being "rose-colored" all the time is not a good thing unless you know when to correct. Today, I take off my "rose-colored glasses" and look through a different-colored lens when I feel I am being one-dimensional.

Looking at life with different lens allows you to view situations from many perspectives, including both microscopic and telescopic views. It also means looking at something from all angles and from new angles.

To look at any situation from a new lens or from a different angle, you must be able to clear your mind. Open your mind to new information and getting that information from new sources, including trees and streams.

Why do I want to look through a new lens, and why is that so important? When you are able to look at a situation with new or different lenses, the pool of available solutions expands.

Some individuals make excellent problem solvers because they are able to look at many options and apply the option that best fits. This skill may come naturally for some individuals, while others have to work at brainstorming ideas, solutions, and actions.

Being able to brainstorm or look for multiple solutions to a problem allows us to go with the flow. It is like watching the water in a river flow by. Whether it moves around a rock, either left or right, it is still moving downstream. In life, there may be multiple routes to go "downstream" and there may be detours, but if you know you have choices and are able to move with the flow, you can quickly make a decision and move forward. It allows us to change the perspective that "there is only one solution to a problem and if you do not find that one solution, you will fail." Once you understand that you have options, you do not feel trapped. You find information that you did not previously have, and with this new information, you are able to make better decisions.

This ability is this important because it allows us to move through life without always trying to control everything we do and everything others do. It gives us tools to be flexible and continue to move forward. We move with the natural flow of earth's energy, and it becomes easier to do so. As individuals, being flexible and adaptable is important in our daily lives. In today's world, where our economy is struggling and jobs are hard to find, we must be able to look at the same situation in new light. In many jobs, we are being asked to do more with less time and fewer resources. We must look for new ways to address old issues or ways to work more efficiently.

When we are able to view situations from multiple angles, we become lifelong learners. We are not stuck in one path, one route, and one way of doing things. We change with those around us, including Mother Earth and her changing landscape. We change with the youth who are entering the workforce and adults who are leaving the workforce. We flow with time and the energy associated with time and change.

We can get into situations where we spend *too* much time looking at the same situation from different angles or different lens. This means we are stuck in our heads and are not listening or acting with our heart. We learn to interpret information in a new manner, and that brings freedom and learning. The energy that we have today is different than what we had when we were ten years old, and it will be different when we are eighty years old. How we look through our lens will need to change for us to live successfully within this space we call earth. We will be able to create great shifts in our lives. These shifts allow us to move through changes along our journey with more speed and confidence.

Connection with Heart

I frequently coach people to "be in the heart versus being in the head," and many people do not understand what I mean. We all know our hearts do not think! I know some of the best analytical-minded people in the IT field, and I know that they can analyze anything and everything and then reanalyze. In the end, they do not make a decision or make multiple decisions because they understand that there are multiple methods to solving a problem. If you take the time to analyze all the options and but never make a decision, that is in itself making a decision. The decision is the subconscious message to "not take any action." The analytical thinking and conversations are answers from the head, not from heart. To "live through the heart" means "listening to the heart" for messaging and direction and acting from the heart. This is counter to how we have been taught to maneuver through life with thought-based actions. We go to school to learn to use the brain, not feel with the heart. Think of writing a term paper, where you start with a theory or an idea. You write the outline (when I wrote this book, I started with an outline), all analytical and purposeful. We have conditioned ourselves to make decisions from the head. Thus, we prevent ourselves from making decisions based on our hearts. Listening to your heart is often thought to be done only in romance novels or old movies. We are now in a time that we are being asked to live through and act from our heart. All our energy comes from center and from our heart, so would we not want to listen to that heart energy as the action to take? When you are able to distinguish between thoughts and actions that come from the head and those that are heartfelt, you have another lens to look at life. When you are able to look at a situation from the heart, and decide action from the heart, it is a pure answer and an action that should be considered.

Listening to and acting upon your heart means acting from a feeling of love. This often is different from acting from an analytical place. When we act from our heart and from a place of love, it brings joy.

Practicing
A favorite activity I do with clients is the practice of talking to trees. This may sound silly, but I challenge you to try it. A tree is a library of knowledge. There is such wisdom in trees—they have seen changes in their living spaces, and they have felt change in their roots as the land and water shifts below. They have a bird's-eye view of events that we can only see from an airplane. Talk to a tree, and see what information is shared.

I have a favorite mystical place, near the river in Minnesota, that I like to hike with my children. My son took me to this area when he felt the tree energy. As we hiked, we noticed many of the old oak trees had face-like bark. We giggled and pointed to the grouchy features in one and the tree that appeared to have a perpetually open mouth. We stopped to share what each of us felt with each tree. I was, and am to this day, drawn to one particular wise tree, and I can feel the peace rise up into my body when I stand beneath him. I am sure that I am standing on his solid roots, and the peace I feel is his energy rising up in the ground. He welcomes me to the forest. He does not have many visitors, so he is appreciative when we come and acknowledge his presence. Some come and never say anything to the trees, bypassing them as if they were not living at all. Isn't that interesting that a living thing would want to be acknowledged as a living thing? I gently touch this magnificent tree and thank him for being there and for the wisdom he has shared today. I ask him to continue to watch out for the trees in that area and that he continue to share his wisdom.

For your exercise, find your tree. This may be a tree that is in your front or back yard, or it may be a tree that is along one of your favorite hiking trails. Quiet your mind. For thousands of years, our ancestors sought knowledge from the earth and all that is here; why would you not do this? Introduce yourself, and thank this tree for being with you today. Is your tree female or male? Do not doubt yourself. If you feel a female presence, your tree is a female, and you may ask her name. If you feel your tree has a male presence, you may ask him his name. Listen and feel with your heart. This is connecting at a "soul" and base level, not to connect with an analytical brain.

Notice how you feel at this time. Do you feel joyous, serious, or that you want to laugh? This is the feeling emanating from your tree friend. Notice how you feel in your body and if you have any aches, pains, or twitches. Does your tummy growl? Do you feel pressure in your head, or are you thirsty? These are all elements of your tree friend that you are feeling. Notice how *your* body is feeling and what impressions you are picking up. If you feel thirsty, ask your tree friend if he or she is thirsty. Do you hear a response?

Is your tree giving you any visuals, such as moving branches? Are you drawn to any leaves that appear brighter in color than others? Are there birds now singing? Are they also drawn to your tree? Notice the activities around you, and become part of that environment.

When we moved to a new home a number of years ago, we had a tree in the front yard that did not want to be there. It was a sole tree. Each time I drove into the driveway, I was greeted with a feeling that he did not want to be there. He was unhappy and lonely.

He was a good-sized crab apple tree, and I felt that he would do better in the back yard rather than near our busy street. I did not share this feeling with anyone, as at that time, I thought they would think I was crazy. I did talk to my neighbor who happened to have a successful landscaping business. I asked him if he could replace the tree with a maple tree and take this tree to a location like in a back yard. The neighbor replaced the tree and put him in his back yard.

Today, I can look at him from my deck, and he appears happy, and this makes me happy. Each spring, he is now full of blossoms. He has the privacy and the quietness of a back yard. Our maple is bold and beautiful, and each fall, he hosts the most beautiful red leaves in the neighborhood. As I remember this tree, I am happy that I moved into that home and was able to move the tree so that he could have a fulfilled life. Does that sound silly? Not anymore!

Interpreting Your Messages

When you are able to hear messages or gain information from a new venue (such as nature or your heart), how do you decipher the message? What other questions would you like to ask your tree friend? He or she is an impartial bystander and can often supply amazing information when you are silent and listen with your heart.

At one time, when I was visiting my tree, I distinctly heard him say that he would help my son decide how he would approach school. I had been worried about my son and what direction he may take with school. I had not asked my tree what I could do to help my son, but my tree seemed to know that I was worried. It was the most amazing feeling when I had this giant of a tree tell me that he would help my son. I have never shared this conversation that I had with this oak tree with my son, but I do know that my son's most favorite place to hike is near this tree. I have seen him sit and look at this oak tree and whatever conversations they are having are between them. Perhaps it is only the tree counseling him, but whatever it is, we always feel more at peace after those hikes.

During the winter months, my son often talks about the summer walks and anticipating being able to walk along the river. We talk about how we did not do that enough last summer and vow to do more in the upcoming months. Now that the river has flooded, we drive past the trail heads and wonder how our trees are doing. How they will feel this summer once the water has subsided? We are anxious to visit them again.

> Where is your tree?
> Who is your tree?
> What do you feel when you are in the presence of your tree?
> What messages do you hear, feel, sense?
>
> *Let go of past beliefs, and let go while you talk to your tree!*

Chapter 5: Courage

Say "Yes" with Trust and without Fear

On my second trip to Sedona, I went with the intent of saying "yes" to anything that Indiana Griffon suggested or threw at me. This was brave, and as I think back, I do not fully understand why I was driven to this decision to boldly say yes. I normally spent time planning and thinking through my actions and operated from a viewpoint of taking an action only when I knew the outcome. This trip was different. I wanted to experience the new and unknown, and I trusted that the universe would help me expand my perception of who and how I *am* in the world. I needed to get out of my comfort zone in the areas that I felt I could control, and allow myself to grow.

I wanted to sleep outside on the rocks of Sedona. I do not know why, it was something I had to do. I ask Indiana Griffon if he could recommend someone that provided that service in Sedona. He had spent many years hiking and camping, and he suggested the ruins of a shaman. (a holy Native American or a medicine Native American). He said that it was a longer hike, but I did not care.

Prior to my trip, my friends were worried about me. They told me about snakes, scorpions and tarantulas. My dad shared stories of a time he was stationed on a Marine base in the desert and walked the perimeter at night, often coming upon snakes. I heard the reservation in his voice as he asked me, "Are you sure you want to do this?" I truly love my friends, but they held the fear, whereas I had none. I had no experience with snakes, scorpions, or tarantulas and was determined that I was not going to take on fears from others. My intent was to say "yes" without fear and that meant trusting those around me to keep me safe and trusting myself. I had to believe that spirit was not going to put me in a place of danger when the drive to take this trip was so strong. I was proud of myself for acting upon an unknown when it felt like it was the right thing to do. I would never recommend taking unsafe actions, but I would recommend to check your fears. In this case I was in good hands, and really had no reason to fear anything.

We began our hike as the sun was starting to set. As we made our way through the trees, Indiana Griffon forgot something in his vehicle and while he ran back to where he'd parked, he left me alone in the middle of the trees. For a moment, I wondered if he would return and quickly told myself that was a silly thought. My cell phone rang, and it was my brother, calling to chat. When he asked where I was, I said I was in the middle of the woods at the base of a mountain I was about to climb and would then camp for the night. There was a long pause, followed by his comment that he did not think that was a smart thing to do and I might want to rethink that decision. It was too late; there was nothing to rethink.

As I said goodbye to my brother with a promise to call him in the morning, Indiana Griffon returned, and we continued on our way. By the time we neared the shaman's cave, it was dark. I had a flashlight and offered to give it to him, but he said that we would climb by the light of the full moon and that was all we needed. That was my first moment of panic. WHAT? Hike in the dark? I began to think about snakes, scorpions, and tarantulas, all those creepy crawlers that my friends had planted in my mind. All their fears and stories came vividly flooding into my head. Was I crazy? I took a deep breath and continued hiking.

Indiana Griffon carried the sleeping bags, pillows, and so on. I carried my camera and about eight bottles of water in my backpack. As we climbed, I noticed the sloshing of the water. The weight of it made me pay attention to how my body was moving around prickly bushes, downed trees, and anything else I could not see. I refrained from turning on my flashlight, as tempting as it was.

Chapter 5: Courage

As we neared a ridge, Indiana Griffon told to wait while he took his packs to the cave and he would come back for me. He told me there was a ledge with a good drop off, and I would need to inch along the ledge, hugging close to the wall of the mountain. He again said to stay put and he would be right back. I stood in the dark on this ledge, unable to see how far down the drop was. My mind told me that it was miles, my body began to shake. As we inched along the ledge, I tried to regain calmness and thought all was under control until my supporting leg slid out from underneath me on some loose rocks. My heart went into cardio-workout-levels, and I started shaking again. The eight bottles of water felt like eight gallons of water, and their weight made my backpack slosh from side to side and was about to take me backward and over the side of the mountain. I asked him to stop for a few moments so that I could calm my mind and body. I did not tell him that my legs were shaking uncontrollably. I did not want him to know that I was scared, and I did not want to believe that this was not a good idea after all. I took another deep breath and threw my trust into the universe thinking, "If I fall, I fall," and at that moment, I knew I would not fall. We pushed on and made it safely to the cave.

How often do we turn back out of fear? How often do we just give up because shaky legs become too much for us to bear? How often do we push through fear and blindly trust that all is as it is supposed to be and that, in the end, there will be an amazing growth or experience?

I felt the cave close in on me. When I did drop into a deep sleep, I had the most amazing dreams. When I opened my eyes the next morning, I could not believe the view before me. I was above the tree tops looking out over a valley. It was a beautiful morning, high on the mountain. As we began our descent, we came to the ledge I had been stuck on the previous night. The drop was not that bad at all. If I would have fallen, I would have been bruised or scratched but would have been fine. Nature again provided me a valuable lesson: "It is not as bad as our mind wants us to believe." We have stories twirling around in our heads that often prevent us from experiencing the moment and the growth opportunities those moments present.

Many of us speculate how a situation will play out before the event happens. The shaking in my legs was expended energy, and energy that I did not need to give up. I did not need to have that moment of panic or fear. Do not speculate until you know, as doing so only builds protection walls around you. Putting light on the situation illuminates the real, or unreal, danger. In this case, daylight was enough to show me there were no danger at all. The fear was all in my mind and based only on what I thought were there.

Building a Security Wall

We are surrounded by devices that provide security: security alarms, security guards, security cameras, security blankets, and security dogs. There are security mechanisms on our computers, our cars, and our homes, and security tracking devices implanted in our pets. We read magazines and books about security, and we talk about feeling secure in our relationships and careers. All these are based on the premise of protection and security. When these security mechanisms are broken or breached, we become upset and often do not understand how the failure happened. We may increase the security to build another layer of protection. Who or what are we protecting ourselves from? Most security mechanisms are meant to protect us from ourselves, and the reality is that we are our biggest offenders. We build fears in our minds and protect ourselves with energetic armor that others can often find impossible to penetrate.

There is a universal movement to live in elevated, and lighter levels of energy and love. This includes living without fear. We contradict the laws of this energy by locking our light and locking our hearts. We build walls around ourselves, effectively restraining *all* our movements and our ability to feel love. We believe that by being protected and secured, we are secure when, in fact, we are alone and isolated. We want love, relationships, and the freedom to love, but we expend energy to keep ourselves protected from what we say we want.

Feeling pure love can be described as basking in a "heated flow of honey." It warms our soul and fills all the nooks and crannies in all dimensions of our being. It is pristine, and some may call it a higher love or energy light. We long for it, seek it, do crazy things to achieve it, but we stop short or prevent ourselves from openly experiencing it. We block ourselves with an armor of security that *nothing* can penetrate.

Because love is energy, and we are energy, when we block the flow of love, our energy stops. We create roadblocks that slow or prevent us from moving forward. Life, career, relationships, and simply being are struggles, and our actions feel forced rather than easy. We know we must love ourselves before others can love us, but we also need to *allow* love to flow before any energy can *leave* or flow *to* us.

Why do we consciously or unconsciously block our energy? Why do we guard our hearts and emotions in an armored box that keeps us in a secure, sterile place? Why do we arm ourselves with emotional security alarms, guards, and cameras that are always on and ready to alert us to the danger of letting our guard down? Why expend so much energy on protecting against something that we think might happen?

These security systems are built upon perceived fears or history-based fears. Memories of emotional pain keep us locked in that moment, and we remember the pain or the perceived memory of pain. We easily forget the feeling of love. We often choose pain or anger, and the fear of the pain, holding onto anger, and avoidance of love prevents us from feeling that creamy-dreamy-energy that makes us believe we can do and be anything. This energy is the most powerful energy we have available to us to. It is the energy that moves, motivates, and masters our dreams. I am not talking about romantic movie love; I am talking about pure love and operating in all that we do from a place in the heart: true heart love. This includes interactions with the teller at the bank, the grocery cashier, and the dentist. It includes peers, employees, and teammates. It includes family, friends, and those we hold closest to our hearts.

When we lock-down our greatest energy, we slow down, and others around us slow down. How we are motivated, what we accomplish, and how we feel is diminished or stopped. We intuitively know this, yet we continue to operate from a place of fear or anger, and not pure love.

Exercise

Getting back to a place of operating from love, and in love, focus on opening your heart. Pay attention to when you are in fear or operating from a point of anger.

What fear blockers have you put in place?

What security walls or protection fields have you built?

What would you like to do, but fear prevents you from taking action?

Breathe and think of a huge light in the center of your chest, pulsing outward. Choose your color of light—it can be white, pink, green, blue, or violet—and hold it there. See it expanding, pulling in universal energy, and pulsing back out ten times stronger. See what happens when you try this exercise with family, friends, and children, and in large crowds. Pull and hold the light. Think of this light pushing away and filling the space where your fear or anger was. Did you feel this fear or anger in your head, chest, and belly? Feel this light move into that space. Use this light to dispel dead or stale energy such as fear or anger. Focus, breathe, and smile. Feel this fresh, new energy, and pay attention to how the energy of those around you has shifted.

What Happens When You Say No to the Flow?
When I hold classes, I never turn people away. If people cancel, I do not get upset. I feel this aligns with the flow of the universe. If someone is not able to attend the class, she is not meant to be there at that time, and the more appropriate time may or may not present itself.

There is a natural flow to how our lives flow each day. Each day, I try to operate with ease and grace, meaning that if something I am doing does not seem to flow or it feels like a struggle, I am going against the natural flow of energy.

If you have ever tried to walk into a stadium as the fans are exiting, you know this feeling. Each step is a bump into someone or a maneuver that forces you to shuffle left or right. You must stop and start again, and it feels like it takes forever to get to where you need to be. This "moving against the flow" and is like saying "no" to the flow.

Like energy in the universe, there is a natural flow in our lives. When we are in this natural flow, all seems to be working well as we move through our days with ease and grace. When we are not in flow, our days feel like we are walking the wrong way in a crowd.

This is a strong message to stop and notice what is moving in the wrong direction or is "in the wrong lane" of our life. Most of us continue to battle with this movement upstream instead of pausing to assess what is happening and what other methods might we use to correct the flow.

I was once in a position where I dreaded getting up in the morning and going into the office. I was tired, and crabby; it felt like my brain did not want to function. I was not engaged. I worked crazy hours but never felt that I was making progress. By all standards, I should have been happy. I was productive, but the job was not something I wanted to do, and I wasn't enjoying it. I was expending a tremendous amount of energy to the point that my weekends were largely spent rejuvenating. One day, over coffee with a friend, I found myself first verbalizing that I wanted something new and that I was burned out. My friend was surprised. Outwardly, all was fine, and I was living the American dream. Within six weeks, I was in a new job and was newly energized. When I look back over that and other times in my career, there is a pattern where I got into the wrong "swim lane" or the lane changed and was no longer a fit. I stayed too long in the lane and expended all my energy maintaining, without ever moving forward. The moment I switched lanes to something that fit better with my swim style, I felt renewed energy and was excited about where I was going and what I was doing.

When things feel like they are a push or a struggle, pay attention to what is happening around you. When you get in the right "swim lane" or move with the energy flow, and all is going well, pay attention to how this feels. You will feel excited and energized about what you are doing. When you are in the flow of energy, it is steady and strong. You know you are outside of the flow of energy when it begins to slow or waiver. When our energy begins to decline, we try to put more energy toward it to reengage and to regain that feeling of being in the flow. Sometimes that works, but more often it is a message that something has shifted or changed. We are always evolving. If we do not evolve with the changes, we are no longer part of the flow and stop learning. We must shift, or our actions must shift, for the new flow.

The moment you say "no" to the natural flow, it feels sluggish and tiresome. I tell my clients that when you are in the flow, the flow happens. It feels effortless, and there is rightness about it. As you continue to say yes to this flow, it expands into a natural flow that fuels your energy reserves.

Exercise

Where in your life are you relative to the flow of natural energy? Does life feel effortless and easy?

Where in your life are you outside the natural flow?

The universe sends us messages all the time, but most often we are not attuned to the meaning. We reason away the message, and we call ourselves crazy, stupid, or silly for hearing a message that we believe to be out of the norm. We forget that we get to create this every moment.

Letting Go
Through my years of executive management and later in coaching, I often found myself telling people to let go. I was often met with comments like these:

"I can't."
"I don't know how."
"That's impossible for me to do."
"I tried that once and I'll never do that again."
"I have to be in control."
"I like control."
"That's the way I am."

Fear causes us to hang onto what no longer serves us—fear of the unknown, fear of what that it would feel like if we totally relinquished control. Would it surprise you to know that we have no control over anything? Many people spend their entire lives trying to create and control a lifestyle that is always going against the flow. They are always swimming upstream.

Emerging Energy

In my mountain climb to the shaman's cave, there was a moment when I let go. I stopped trying to control, and I relinquished my fear and panic feelings to the divine. Once I did that, the shaking in my body stopped, my energy was turned inward to my body, and I was able to move on.

It is like watching children fight sleep. They get crabby, cranky, and sometimes cry. Their heads bob as they fight sleep, trying to stay awake, until they finally give into the *need* to sleep.

Sometimes we fight to maintain control when we need to relinquish control for the *need* to reserve or regain our energy levels. When we go with the flow, our energy is aligned, and we are able to maintain a consistent level of energy. We often must let go to continue with this flow. Letting go is a foreign concept to many people, particularly if they have built their lives around being in control.

People who fear snakes, scorpions, tarantulas, heights, flying, or public speaking want to control their outcomes and their feelings in situations where there is nothing to control. If you let go and can be with the situation, you maintain the flow of energy with forward momentum, ease, and grace. When you believe that all will be as it should be, you are more likely to let go than if you fight the experience.

Most often, you spend energy before an event and after an event, replaying over and over in your mind what happened and what you would do differently if you could do it all over again. This is wasted energy. The event was what it was, and the next moment will also be a new moment with a new experience.

Chapter 6: Filling in the Gap

Are You in "Monkey Brain" Mode?

Earlier, we talked about busy brains, and this is often termed "monkey brain." Many of us find it difficult to quiet our mind and clear the clutter. We live in a culture that moves at lightning speed, and the expectation that we maintain this speed is reinforced each day. The need to move faster, be better, and do it all quicker has become the norm. We have to relearn to *be* versus *doing* all the time. In Chapter two, we discussed the importance of clearing away old information to create clean space and fill it with new information. To clear unneeded information from our thoughts, we need to understand how our thought process works.

When people tell me that they are unable to meditate because they are unable to clear their thoughts, and they quickly gave up. This idea that we must quickly know how to do something is also a cultural expectation. Many of us have forgotten how to learn. Many of us do not know how to relinquish control and let go of the expectation that we will know and that we must learn, or in some cases relearn, some behaviors.

I tell many of my clients that the fact they were not able to meditate the first time they tried is not a reason to give up. They need to let go of the thought that meditation is not doing anything and therefore is not valuable. They do not see the "productive output" from quiet time. Do you think that you can shut off your thought patterns so that you are thinking absolutely nothing? If you are thinking nothing, you have no brain waves. You are always thinking something, even if you think about telling your body to take deep breaths. Focusing on your breathing is a way to redirect thought, calm runaway thoughts, or stop spinning in circles.

Another way to meditate on a solution to a problem is to think about that problem while you close your eyes and relax. Many people find this difficult, and it takes practice. To believe that you will feel comfortable doing this the first time is an unfair expectation. If you can do it, great, as you are on your way to assisting your mind in quieting itself.

The point of meditation on an issue or problem and seeking an answer is to provide connection to the etheric realm. The etheric realm includes layers of space that contain energy and information that we are able to tap into for information. It allows us to connect to other dimensions of information not available to us when we are scattered in our energies.

Sometimes I lay with my eyes closed and let my thoughts race to see where they take me. Eventually, my thoughts tire, and sometimes I get my answer on the end of the mind-ramble. There is no right or wrong way for our brains to work. We have only the brain and nothing to compare it to, other than to listen to others and decide how a normal brain should function. We must remember that we are all individuals and our experiences may be similar, the same, or totally different from those of the people around us. How we experience a situation is based on the reference points in our life, our past, and the openness we allow ourselves.

I was asked recently about "soul travel." Soul travel, also known as astral travel or astral projection. It is when your soul continues its work in the ethers while you are sleeping. Simply stated, it is the belief that it is a state of mind/being you achieve when your consciousness merges with your soul to which then you slowly begin to move away from the physical body outwards. It may travel to another country, city, or home and help or teach someone there. It may do education for its own benefit, or it may repair or help with earthly or etheric events. It may even be going to a soul party. There are large gaps of time during our sleeping hours, and many people dream vivid dreams and wonder if they actually lived them.

Some like to explain this as the soul leaving the body and following a gold or silver thread out into the universe. When it is done it, follows that gold or silver thread back to your body. I question the importance of following a thread outside our body. I believe this is a visual or explanation that we have applied for a reference point. I believe this alleviates the fear that we might leave and not find our way back. Being tethered to our body is how we know that we will return. There is safety in knowing you will get back into your body and not land somewhere else. Is your mind or energy moving while everything within you remains intact? Again, soul travel is the easy explanation and provides a visual to help us understand something for which we have no reference.

This in itself is building a reference. When we obtain information for which we do not have a reference point, we build a new record. It's like going to the library. When new books or material are added, they are indexed, logged, cataloged, and put on the shelf to be checked out later. Memory does this for us; it logs information in a reference location so that we can retrieve it later. What happens when it's a new reference and we don't know how to catalog or categorize it? We have to have a solution to how it is logged. We have to have logic where sometimes there is no logic. We expend huge amounts of energy speculating and filling in the gaps when we do not know.

Old Reference Points

At any given moment, we have an opportunity to recreate. You may think of these moments as do-overs or mulligans, but regardless, they are opportunities to pause, think, and set a new direction. Many individuals use these times to do exactly what they just did. These become the déjà vue of life experiences.

Sameness means comfort, and we like living in comfort. Others are numb to what has happened and are not aware that *they* have the power to manifest something new in any area they desire. The laws of the universe have us reliving or redoing situations over and over again until we learn the life lesson or until we decide that we are done and declare completion. Once we take that step, we are free to move in a new direction. When we move in this new direction, we are *awake*. An "awake moment" is the "ah-ha" moment when we feel clear about who we were and what we were doing, knowing that a situation did not work for us and consciously deciding to live differently. We are the force that will change us.

In my twenties, I remember a period of dating the "same men." I call them same men, because though I knew none were right for me, I continued to attract and fall in and out of relationships with them. I was frustrated with always achieving the same results while believing that I was adjusting who I was looking for. I remember laying on the floor in my living room, crying, writing in my journal that this was the universe trying to show me a life lesson, and knowing that until I learned that life lesson, I would forever continue in this cycle. I remember writing, OKAY, I GOT IT, NOW LET ME MOVE ON!! The truth was that I did not "have it," and the universe was not going to let me move on until I figured it out.

This repetition of dating the same type of man was not aligned with my philosophy, and the spinning felt like wasted energy. Not sure how to leave the cycle, I stopped dating and focused on my career, traveling, and exercise regime. I began to meet real men of substance and the relationships brought marriage and then children. I learned my most valued lesson. I had lost myself, and the "spin time" was the universe directing me to pay attention to *me*. When I was not paying attention to myself, I lost myself and my goals. The goals of marriage and kids were foreign but felt right for that next phase of my life, or what I now call my next lesson. I realize now that when I moved into that phase, it further allowed me to lose myself or hide. I was so busy for the next eighteen years with my family, kids and career that I did not emerge until I let go and said, "Enough." Once I did this, I found me again.

There are many lessons in life, and we must remember that we chose to come to earth to have these adventures (lessons), so we should expect challenge and growth, knowing that when we don't grow and feel frustrated, the universe is telling us to stop, focus, and learn these lessons:

- Set your goals with purpose and commitment.

- Do not lose yourself while achieving a goal.

- Do not focus on a goal that is not your own.

- If you feel you are in a "do-again" situation, stop and learn the lesson.

- Once you have learned the purpose, you will freely move in another direction.

Many people live an entire lifetime redoing an event, relationships or situation because they are not awake in their living. Focus on being awake and alert, and know how your knowledge banks and reference libraries are created.

Knowledge Banks and Reference Libraries

Every memory and experience becomes an element logged in our knowledge bank, like an entry in the registry in our brains. I am often asked how I started as an intuitive reader, how did I learn, and when did I start talking to my guides and angels. I was born with them, and until recently, my first memory was around sixth grade. I remember slumber parties and staying up late into the night talking about ghosts, reading horoscopes, and wishing that we could see into the future. I hated funeral homes and graveyards but, at that time, did not understand the energy I was picking up. Later, I dabbled with astrology and channeling information. I sat and drew circles as information came to me. At that age, I did not know what to do with the information and without a support system to expand or use this gift, I hid it from everyone except a select few friends. Like most kids, I did not want to be odd. Recently, as I was teaching a class, I was explaining my background when a memory came to me so vividly that it caused me to paused midsentence. This memory was from second grade, and it was my earliest memory of hearing messages from angels. At that moment I'd gone back earlier in my knowledge bank.

Have you heard the phrase "he's a walking dictionary?" There is truth to that phrase in that we are all walking dictionaries and reference libraries. The dictionaries that we hold within us are our own, as we built them. We are born with a brain that can compute and process information far greater than most large-scale computers. We use only a small fraction of our capacity, and what we store and retain for future use is at our own discretion.

Each experience or event allows us to expand our library and reference material. Each event also allows us to delete or recatalog this information. In my example of questioning about angels, I recataloged that knowing into an area that needed further research.

I am training a new member of our household. Meeko is a twelve-week old, black-gray tabby kitty and a daredevil. If he were a child, I'd be running around after him providing a safety net and afraid that he would hurt himself. Meeko is learning what "no" means as I am training him to not jump up on things. He is learning how to live in this house, and I am relearning how to live in this house with a new member. We are both logging new information or modifying old information each day.

I have another five-year-old cat named Ollie. Ollie enjoys hanging out and not hanging *on* things. He has never had a new kitty in his house. He had an older brother, but he now gets to be an older brother to Meeko, and he does not like this much, as he tells us each opportunity he gets by his low, guttural growls and hissing. He has turned grumpy.

It has been interesting watching these cats. Meeko came from a litter of five and he continues to approach Ollie fully expecting him to openly accept him. I can almost hear him say, "I'm just like you, come play with me." That is Meeko's reference point. His knowledge bank contains happy days with his siblings, playing hard, wrestling, and then curling up for naps. His reference point is "HEY, HERE'S ANOTHER CAT!" Ollie's knowledge bank contains mellow moments of curling up on the bed or in a corner of the closet. His reference point may be with our elder cat that died last winter. In that relationship, Ollie was the aggressor. Perhaps Ollie is seeing a change in his kingdom? Like most humans, he likes his old reference points and does not do well with change.

Over time, both cats will adjust in their own fashion. Both of them will build new and expanded knowledge banks. I fully believe that Meeko will learn his boundaries, and I also believe that Ollie will adjust to his new boundaries. Sometimes through a life event or change, we are forced to expand our knowledge banks, and like it or not, we adjust.

How we adjust depends on how we look at our circumstances, our willingness to change, and how deeply we attempt to hold on to the past. We also build other reference points in our libraries. Let's say that am going to try meditation. I begin to build a knowledge base of what meditation is based on what I have read or been told and what I expect meditation should be all about. I log that information as my reference point. When I try meditation, I measure my experience against those reference points and adjust them. Each person builds his own perspective of what meditation is and logs it. Feeling good about the experience and feeling emotions such as joy, peace, and laughter all raise your vibration, and you are more apt to want the experience again. If I should have a bad experience, or what I do experience is not what I expected and I feel I've failed or did not do it correctly, it may leave a lower vibration, and I will not be as ready to try again. If I have a reference in my knowledge bank that I have had other new activities that I tried, didn't like, tried a few more times, and felt better, I may set that reference point as a new expectation. These lower vibration points of reference are what keep us from trying an activity again. Most of us do not like doing something that is uncomfortable!. We can be tough on ourselves with setting expectations and comparisons. We compare ourselves to others, to past experiences, even to expectations of events we have not yet experienced. We may stop ourselves from trying anything, because we expect to fail.

In my panic attack about scuba diving in Brazil, I pulled a reference point from something I had not done yet. Why did I put up a roadblock for something I had never experienced but was afraid of? I had a past experience of being in public in a swimsuit and not feeling comfortable at that time. I had a fear of not being able to breathe under water, yet I was well trained prior to the dive and the depth of the dive was relatively shallow. I have a pool in my back yard, so I am not afraid of water, nor do I have a fear of being in a swimsuit, yet I created my own roadblock for something that could be totally amazing! In both good and bad experiences, we may keep repeating the same situation with another person or another event. We sabotage our lives out of fear. We may know that a certain type of relationship is not right for us, but we continue to choose the same behaviors in different partners.

Why Do We Keep Going Back for the Wrong Answer?
Because we do not like change or fear the unknown, changing our patterns can mean fear. Sometimes we remain in a situation because we know it, and that feels safer than the unknown.

Another reason for repeating or choosing sameness is that our knowledge reference points have not been reset. We go to our knowledge base and see the reference point, know in our heads that it is not the best, yet we continue to use it.

In corporate manufacturing, many organizations use six-sigma methods to change processes, measure success, and move from a one-time change to processes for continuous improvements. The levels of proficiency in this methodology include Green Belts and Black Belts. This methodology is meant to help an organization learn from present or past and improve it for the future. Individuals do not have a "six-sigma process" to look at events in their lives and improve them. They may settle and be happy with the status quo. If they are not happy, what is their process for stepping back, going internal to assess what happened, learning, and updating their knowledge base? Once they see patterns, they can adjust their behaviors and expectations.

Exercise

What events or experiences do I repeat when I don't want to?

- How many times have I repeated these events?
- Take ten minutes and rewrite this history to create new knowledge and reference points.

When have I sabotaged something and later regretted it, or when have I knowingly have set myself up for lesser performance?

- Take ten minutes and write about the behaviors that prevented you from taking action.

Get Out of Your Head, Think with Your Heart

Now that you have done the above exercise and thought through what you have learned or are learning about yourself, it is time to get out of your head and get into your heart. This is termed "thinking from your heart," and it will push you to act upon feelings rather than acting upon what is in your head. We have been programmed by others' definitions of success. In Western society, we have worked very hard for success with a career and acquiring a home, a car, and other possessions. Some of these possessions provide entertainment, and in some cases, they provide us joy, with that joy, there is also loss. Time to *be*, to enjoy events that bring us joy, and simple things without all the bells and whistles are lost. We sit behind desks, workstations, or in production centers operating from our brains, not moving our bodies and not exercising our hearts. How do we *feel* each day? What excites us, motivates us, bring us joy? *Those* are the activities that raise our vibration levels. When we raise our vibration levels, we live in joy.

Meditation is one way to bring us back to the center, which is our beginning. It is the love and the light that we have at our core that motivates and drives us. If we tap into this energy, we have infinite resources at our finger tips, but doing so requires us to get out of our head and stop analyzing everything that we think we are supposed to do. Stop trying to create the person you are not, and look within at the perfection that is there.

Chapter 7: Seek Others for Help

Going From Internal to External

Each time I sat down to write this chapter, I had writer's block. It was the Fourth of July, and I allowed myself to sleep in later than normal, intending to write as soon as I woke up. I assumed that I would be refreshed and ready to write, but I sat at my computer and looked at the gorgeous Minnesota sunshine. I contemplated doing a drumming meditation using the deerskin drum that I had just purchased or going for a walking meditation. I allowed myself an hour for this distraction, promising to get back to work once I was back at the house. Walking was always a great way to clear my thoughts or release pent-up energy.

I was unsure of where to walk that morning. My old hiking grounds were replaced by houses, and a new road had been installed through the surrounding wetlands. These were the areas where turkeys always left me feathers, and I often shared the same trails with deer as they ran between fields. Hawks often called from the tree tops, and if I was lucky, I saw a fox or two. I preferred these walks to walking the sidewalks of the neighborhoods, as I was entertained by the wildlife along my four- to eight-mile walks. On that day, I dreaded the sidewalk but was determined to clear the pent-up energy. I grabbed my iPod shuffle and headed out the door, only to find that the batteries were dead. This was a message that I needed to be within myself for processing and eliminate all external distractions.

I decided to walk the new four-lane road that had been under construction. Barricades blocked cars and other vehicles, but it was perfect for walking, and it gave me a chance to see on foot the changes to a favorite area.

I was hot and thought of the water bottle that I had forgotten on the counter at home. This wasn't the inspirational walk that I had expected. I passed a few bicyclists who were taking advantage of this untraveled road and thought about the afternoon and how I would spend my day. A doe ran in front of me. Yes, she flew across the new, four-lane road, not ten feet in front of me. I was in awe watching how light on her feet she was. I was still standing in awe as her fawn ran in front of me. The fawn was torn between curiosity about me and following her mama. She paused for a second, looked at me, and darted off. A cyclist stopped, and his words broke my thoughts. "Awesome to see that out here isn't it?" "Yes," I said. The new road had not stopped the wildlife from enjoying the trees and wetland. My eyes caught a flock of Canadian geese, and a heron flew by above. Once again, Mother Nature had given me more answers than I had expected.

I continued my walk, grateful for the day. I was even more grateful for these animals that were sending me messages that morning, and I began to process these messages. The deer was a symbol that I had made the right decision on my new drum. The drum had been made by James Michael, and he named it Thunder Bird Wind Drummer. I was meant to have that drum; no more questions on that one.

Thoughts of the deer passing so close to me meant there were more messages for me. Once back at home, I looked up deer in Steven Farmer's book, *Animal Spirit Guides*.[ii]

> "You've been involved in some aggressive, negative circumstance and need to seek out safe, nurturing situations and people. More than ever, you need to trust your gut instinct. You're poised for an enticing adventure, one that will take you down many different paths and lead to many important insights. Be gentle with yourself and others.
>
> The deer is also one of my power animals. You maintain a balance of the masculine traits of mastery, authority,

and protection with the feminine characteristics of love, nourishment, and surrender, yet relate most closely to those associated with your gender. You're highly sensitive and intuitive and are often aware of the feeling of others before they are. You can move with intention, awareness and speed and can change directions quickly while staying completely centered. You're most comfortable outdoors, particularly in the woods or forest, and must frequently spend time w\there to recharge and regenerate"

Mother Nature provides us with hints to our internal being with external messages, but only when we pay attention and listen to them.

When we try to look externally for answers, they are often not there. They are only distractions and temporary replacements for the internal work that we need to do. All our answers come from within. Only we know how we are, what we feel, and how we process joy, happiness, and sorrow. We are all different, and if we look for external answers, we get someone else's answers, not our own.

This requires that you know your internal self. We mask feelings and hide behind careers, relationships, homes, and material possessions that do not fully support who we are internally. We have given up dreams and replaced them with what society says we should have.

All we need is internal, and the external factors are there to support us, not shadow us. When is it safe or practical to move from internal to external, and exactly what does that mean?

In 2011, we experienced a tumultuous year of natural disasters. Many people were impacted by the economy, either by losing a job or becoming overwhelmed with debt as the housing market continued to decline. People walked away from their homes, leaving banks with a portfolio of foreclosed homes. I saw common themes with my clients as they wanted to know what was going on with the weather and the job market and when we would ever "feel normal again." I asked what "normal" was for them.

I saw people forced to leave relationships, homes, or jobs that were not true to their internal being. They were unfulfilled but felt that being in those homes or jobs was better than being alone, not having work, and not having their dream home. This is transformation!

When in transformation, we must go within and find peace within rather than focusing on external circumstances. When you begin to shift your life, start internally and then move external. When I began my internal shift, I changed jobs. I fought to keep the job that kept me exhausted and nearly in tears every day. I look back now and wonder why I fought so hard to make something work that was not meant to be. After having a career and jobs that took me all over the world, I was directed by my guides to remain in Minnesota and focus. I panicked at first, wondering how it would feel to be here, especially in the winter. That first winter, I noticed that even though I had lived in Minnesota all my life, I did not have winter attire and had to shop for warm clothing.

Transformation is not always easy and often not what we expect. I thought I'd learned to let go, but obviously hadn't do so in all domains of my life, and I needed another lesson to just let go. You can have many starts and stops, as I did with my career choices or the years it took to release an unfulfilling relationship.

In transformation, you may find that things that were tolerable are no longer acceptable. When you get off your familiar path, life becomes bumpy, uncomfortable, or painful. You may feel that you are experiencing a run of bad luck. When you are on the right path, you are aligned, and life feels easy. Relationships are easy, and you are able to continue to focus within rather than fighting to maintain an external mask.

> # Exercise
>
> Focus on internal emotions. Notice how you feel when you are at work, with a partner, in your home. Notice if there is an edge, stress, anger, or other low vibrational emotion. If there is, it is time to change something or take action. Sometimes it means going back to the basics or being alone until you find out who you are and what you want.

Leaving Old Habits Behind

I recently worked with a nineteen-year-old college student and prepared myself by calling in some of my protector angels. I normally do not do this, but something spoke to me to call in protection and draw boundaries; only information for the highest divine purpose was allowed to be brought forth. I was wondering who this young man could be that I felt the need to do this. He was a referral from a woman that I had done many readings for, and I trusted her. The first scheduled appointment came and went, and he never showed up. I knew there was fear there for him and that he had been out late the night before and overslept. Later, I got an email from him, asking to set up another time, and apologizing for missing his appointment. I scheduled a time with him and again felt the need to call in my guides in preparation.

When he arrived, I knew that he was going to challenge me, which was necessary for him to believe any of the messages he was to hear. This was often the case for those who came to me and were skeptical. We went to work on his perception of who he was in this life, his nonverbalized goals, and the roadblocks he had purposefully put in his own way. Someday we might read about this young intelligent man as one of our leaders, but to get there he would need to leave behind some of his acquaintances, actions, and behaviors and own his desires for the life he wants to live.

The challenge for me was answering all his questions about dimensional energies, 2012, and God. It ended up being an insightful session for both of us, as we both became students.

The college student could have remained afraid of meeting with me, but something pushed him to seek me out and to get answers to his questions. He needed to hear these messages about his roadblocks. Like many of us, he has great things in store for him if he can trust and *be*.

Who Are Our Roadblocks?
When my son was in high school, I talked to him about expending energy. He spent more time getting out of his assignments than doing them. When he did his school work, he waited until the last day of the weekend and inevitably had to turn down spending time with his friends because he needed to complete his homework.

We all create roadblocks for ourselves. We say "no" when we should say "yes" or believe that we will fail when we have not tried.

It was clear to the college student that he was his own roadblock. He chose to remain friends with two individuals who didn't support nor believe in his dreams. He was attending college to focus on his dream career, and his friends were there to focus on social networking. He needed to make big changes in how he looked at his decisions, as they would impact his future.

When we set up roadblocks, they are often meant to protect us from a perceived pain. We stay in a relationship or in a job because we have adapted to that situation. We settle for mediocre rather than work through our fears and take action.

We are moving to a higher level of energy that demands being a place that is fulfilling and rewarding. It is no longer okay to be in a mediocre anything!

The Universe Steps In

If you don't remove yourself as the road block, the universe steps in.

During a trip to Arizona, I landed in Phoenix and made the drive to my rental in Sedona. It was late, and I didn't want to wake my roommate upon my arrival. Early the next morning, I put on my hiking gear and went hiking, enjoying the fall weather. Though cool, it was still much warmer than Minnesota, and I was in heaven being outside and enjoying being on the land. Indiana Griffon called, and we planned to head down past Phoenix. There was another highly spiritual place he wanted me to experience. Because I was focusing on saying "yes" to all that was thrown at me, I said yes. "What do I need to bring?" I asked. "Sleeping bag, pillow, and towel," he said. This meant we were going to sleep on the land for one or two nights. I had a moment of panic when he said he had set up a sleep site for me and would be less than 100 feet away. I asked about the average weight that a coyote can drag away and held my fear close, not sure how much was teasing and how much was a word of caution. I knew that this would be another first for me to throw a sleeping bag down on the desert and sleep.

The first night passed without incidents. We maintained the fire into the night not for fear of animals or bugs but for the joy of sleeping in the open desert next to a blazing fire, looking at the million stars above. The desert cools off at night, so layers and a warm sleeping bag are necessary. In the morning, we laughed at the number of layers I needed to shed. We had a great day of hiking, and I photographed a number of orbs and one huge violet angel that appeared in the rocks. I thought that I had learned what I needed to learn that day, had put my fears behind, and was ready to wrap it up. We discussed staying another night in the desert or heading back to Sedona. I had made up my mind that I wanted to get back to Sedona to spend at least another day there before heading back to Minnesota. Indiana Griffon wanted to show me one more spot where there was a rock formation that looked like a large skull. I once again said "yes," letting go of my fears.

Emerging Energy

We arrived at our destination, which required a drive off the main road and on a desert trail that wound up and over hills. We passed a dark van where a man sat with his two Rottweilers. We kept driving. We came to the top of a crest, and I was shown the general direction of the skull-rock. I took a few things with me and hiked to the skull, leaving Indiana Griffon behind to bring the food. I gathered wood, made a fire, and spent time meditating. I began to wonder where my hiking partner was. I could hear his van start and then stop in the distance. I knew that he had tried to drive closer to the skull-rock and was stuck in the desert. I walked toward this sound with the small flashlight I'd grabbed at the last minute before leaving Sedona, and I understood why my intuition told me I would need this little light. We had no shovels, and rocking the van back and forth buried it deeper in the dried river bed. We walked to the dark van to ask the man with his dogs if had a shovel we could use. He was a weathered looking man, probably a miner, or so I told myself as he handed the shovels to me with a grin that exposed a toothless smile.

We dug for four hours and were able to dig the van from its hole in the desert, but we had to drive back over the same spot to return to the main road. Once again, the van lodged in the riverbed, and we started to dig again. We knew that we were losing steam. Now the only decision was to sleep at the skull-rock or in the van. Upon Indiana Griffon's urging, while fighting my own internal fear, I opted to join him at the skull-rock. It had a narrow opening, and he took the space deeper in the skull-rock cave. I followed with my sleeping bag and lay with my head near his feet. We both had crazy dreams with crazy images, and both felt that we were visited that night by many elders. I woke in the early morning haze to see a coyote sniffing at my feet—Indiana would not have believed me had I not pointed to the coyote droppings by my feet.

We had survived the night in a skull-rock cave, but we were still stuck. It was my task to see if I could find someone with a four-wheel-drive truck who would be willing to pull us out.

Chapter 7: Seek Others for Help

The first man who tried to help me was not able to get his truck up the hill. He asked how we got over the hill and didn't believe that we were on the right road. He did offer to drive me into town to find a tow service. The nearest town was fifteen miles away, and although I had my cell phone with me, I had no battery left, so I couldn't call Indiana to let him know of my progress. It was Sunday, so I was doubtful I would find a towing service open and I was already starting to think I'd missmy flight home, and would be sleeping another night in the desert. Once in town, a few men quickly offered to help. This was probably the most excitement they'd seen all year.

I never understood the need for dual tired four-wheel-drive trucks, but I was not complaining on that day, and I was happy that the men were willing to help.

I was not comfortable asking for help, much less asking strangers for help. Back to the dirt trail, the men were amused that we'd gone off the road and had dug all night trying to get out. They repeatedly asked me if I was sure I was taking them on the right trail. I began to doubt myself, and we drove over hill after hill until I could see the white van down below. "There," I said. Yes, we probably shouldn't have done it, and yes, we were very stuck. (I am sure our story is told over and over again.) A man who wintered in Arizona was the knight that saved the damsel in the desert. I gave him a kiss on his cheek, some cash for dinner and gas, and waved goodbye. I was able to catch my flight back to Minnesota, and though sad that I was not able to get back to see my friends in Sedona this trip, I needed to process many lessons, one lesson being that I was in the exact spot I needed to be and nowhere else at that moment.

The desert, or some higher powers that be, was not going to let us leave that night. We talked over breakfast that morning and were in awe of how easy it was to be pulled out once we relinquished control, settled in for the night, and went to find help in the morning.

Emerging Energy

I had to knock down many roadblocks on that trip: fear of sleeping in the desert a second night, in a rock-skull, cave, fear of approaching the van guarded by Rottweilers. Fear of walking to find help and not finding anyone. Fear of never getting out of the desert in time to make my flight. This life-defining trip was filled with lessons. It one tested my faith in myself and my ability to remove roadblocks, be in the moment, and remember to be in ease and grace. Digging for four to six hours was not ease and grace; having a dual-wheeler pull us out in five minutes is ease and grace.

To remove roadblocks, they need to be identified. Take the time to process your learning when life throws a challenge at you. (I had a three-hour flight that allowed me to think about what I had just learned.)

Did you identify any roadblocks from the exercise in chapter Six? If you did, you can remove those roadblocks and leave them behind, as they no longer serve you. This allows new practices to replace them.

Exercise

1. **I say "yes" to opportunities and trust that all will align for me. I feel that my life is filled with abundance with these opportunities, and life flows well.**

   If you answered "no" to the above, notice where you say "no" and what answer has just been eliminated. What limitation did you create for yourself? How do you feel about saying "no"?

2. **I do not allow others to influence my actions and decisions when these actions or desires take me away from my desired goal.**

   If you answered "no," why do you allow the influence when it takes you from your desired goal? Do you find you have difficulty stating what you want or difficulty speaking against the beliefs of the majority even when they doesn't match your desired beliefs?

3. **I have people in my life that support me and actively help me remain on track if I derail from my goals.**

   If you answered "no," know that it is important to surround yourself with people who support your goals and help keep you on track when you derail or slow down.

4. **I have practices in place to leave behind old behaviors and start with fresh practices that support my goals and life desires.**

   If you answered "no," it is time to put in place those practices that support your goals and life desires. To focus on these practices may be difficult at first, but once you have focus, you will find your life align with ease and grace.

Continue the Journey; Move or Rust
"Worms will not eat living wood where the vital sap is flowing; rust will not hinder the opening of a gate when the hinges are used each day. Movement gives health and life. Stagnation brings disease and death."—Proverb from traditional Chinese medicine

I love this proverb. Just as a tree has vital sap, we all have vital energy. If we do not keep our energy flowing, it becomes stagnant. Our vibrations slow, and we begin to feel tired, stressed, depressed, and sick. It may become difficult to focus and to move back to a place of fulfillment, joy and happiness..

If we continue our journey toward our goal or desired outcome, we maintain a higher vibration and remain in that place of joy.

We make the choice to move or rust every day. What decisions are you making today, and do they to enable you to move forward?

Chapter 8: Get Over It, Get On With It

Useless Processing of Energy

When I was young, I spent a lot of time with my Grandma Catherine. I spent the day with her when I did not have school. As I got older, I stopped to see her as often as I could. Many times, I drove her to the grocery store to pick up groceries, and she thought she was imposing on my time, but for me, it was a way to drive the car and spend time with her. We laughed about that later and how we perceive about what others think about us. We worry about doing the right thing or avoid asking for help because we don't want to be trouble. It's time to let go, get over it, and get on with it. Have the thought and then release it. Doing so allows you to release that energy.

Again, spirit gives us the opportunity to learn lessons by providing situations to learn. However these situations are not usually what we would call opportunities, nor usually the way *we* think we ought to learn any lessons.

On one of my early travels, I was hiking and camping in the Valley of the Gods in Utah. This amazing area has jutting rocks that rise up from flat desert plains. The rock formations look like sentries or gods, watching over miles of flat land. Though amazingly beautiful, this flat land left little cover for "nature calls." In the middle of the desert, there were no cars driving by, but there is something about privacy or the lack thereof.

As I found the appropriate rock cover, I heard my Grandmother's words, "Just get on with it." I remembered her telling me that there was a point in her life that she realized she'd earned the right to "let go and get on with it." Age brings a sense of what does or does not matter. For her, she'd lived through the Depression Years, raising six children and watching three of the four boys go off to the Marines and the Army during WWII. I don't know exactly what age she declared her freedom from useless processing of energy, but I vowed to take her advice and practice letting go, getting over it, and getting on with it.

My kids are amazing examples of letting go. When something lingers with me and bothers me, my daughter can see it in my face and tells me that I analyze too much. In other words, just get over it. We often have to claim an event, name it, judge it, and then store it in our reference library under "pain." When we look at that reference, we feel the pain over and over again. This is the same as self-torture. It is often easier to define when others take actions that cause pain and wonder why they wallow in it yet do not realize when we do it to ourselves.

Sitting with your feelings, however long you need to sit with them, lets the emotion flow through you—not flow around you, over you, or remain stuck in you. This is naming it, claiming it, and being in the feeling it until the feeling is released. This is letting go. When we get over it, we are able to get on with it. It is a sense of winning the race or earning the Medal of Honor for accomplishment. We can log this process in our reference library as "knowing how to work through emotions in a healthy way."

This Moment

This moment, this time, this place that you are in, is everything. It is all that you need today, tomorrow, and forever; for there is only now. How you are now is all you need.

At any given moment, the universe provides us with all that we need. We often think we should have more, less, or something different from what we have at that moment. We spend time wanting, planning, and dreaming about the future and how to get what we think we need.

There has recently has been more focus on how people are downsizing their homes and possessions. Many of these activities may be driven by the economy. Many large organizations have also focused efforts to right-size or economize their environments and teams. They are looking at where there is excess and reducing or eliminating what is no longer needed. It is relatively easy to reduce or recycle items in our homes. We easily sort closets and drawers and remove items that no longer fit, have not been worn, or are out of style. Professional organizers and professional designers can help us design or organize our closets. By clearing clutter and organizing, we free up space for something new. In organizations, we look for fresh ideas or new methods to tackle an old issue, and by rearranging teams, we can often accomplish this easily. We feel good when we are organized!

In the laws of the universe, when we clean space, we elevate our souls, and this allows us to move to a higher or bigger space. We eliminate that which no longer serves us, allowing us to take on more universal knowledge. This is like cleaning your "karmic space." You clear toxic actions, behaviors, people and events from your life. These actions, behaviors, people, or events drain your spirit and energy, and you have no room for new, healthy energy. It takes effort and practice to clear this space, requires focused time, and is often painful.

To move forward, be aware, be awake, and focus on what you *do* want rather than what you *don't* want. You will move forward quickly when you know what has not worked and what you do not want to repeat. Be aware of toxic foods or behaviors that make your body or mind feel sluggish. Be aware of people and thoughts that are judgmental, reinforce guilt, and don't support freedom, laughter, and joy.

This includes removing reference points to holding pain. The repeat emotions, or emotions that are suppressed and not dealt with, also become toxic to your health and well being.

The universal energies are pushing us hard right now to change. What we have been in the past is no longer serving us, and we must change. The universe pushes us into motion when we do not move fast enough or have chosen not to move. On a physical plane, we believe all is fine, and we've managed to maintain the status quo. However, on a dimensional plane, we all must clear and prepare. If we do not do this on our own, the universe will force us, usually through a major or lingering health issue, loss of a job, or end of a relationship. These events are purposeful, and we should acknowledge them as opportunities to change.

Take a Breath and Go

We all have wishes, dreams, and visions. We often set goals or activities around these wishes, dreams, and visions, but for whatever reason, we often fail to experience them. We get close, or experience a minuscule component, without experiencing the full dream and the joy that accompanies the achievement of a goal. What stops us?

For some, it is fear of accomplishing the goal. For some, it is the belief that they are not worthy to have the dream, and for others, it is the addiction to chasing the dream. We are in love with the dream and always hoping for "someday." What happens when someday never comes? We leave this life looking back in regret, disgust, or a wish for a do-over.

I do not want to get to the point where I have not obtained my dreams. I do not want any regrets. As much as I would like to believe in do-overs and second chances, I am not willing to gamble this lifetime on a what-if scenario.

We all like to feel safe. We like to know what's going to happen, and most of us do not like surprises, but guess what? We have these experiences because we signed up for a lifetime of challenge, excitement, surprise and the ability to create what we want. That includes accomplishing your dreams, goals, and visions. Dream big, and then live those dreams. If you are not living your dream, what do you fear about that dream coming true?

If the problem isn't fear, do you feel worthy of having that experience or obtaining that goal? Are stopped because beliefs that turn to words,

words turn to actions, and actions create failure and disappointment? Do you hear yourself say, "See, I knew I could never do or have this, how stupid of me to even think this would be my reality"? Congratulations; you have just created your own roadblock. You have put into your reality your beliefs, words, actions and validation that you will never accomplish your goal. You have to believe that you are worthy and will achieve your dream. Do not just use words; embody your belief and *live it.*

If you genuinely believe in accomplishment but still are not manifesting your dream, are you in love with the chase? You enjoy talking about it. You like the feeling of wanting something but having it is just beyond your fingertips. You give it one more try, or another month, or invest a bit more, always hoping that the dream will magically happen. You put your energy into wanting rather than living. Might the fantasy be better than accomplishing your goal? What would you do next? Maybe it's not a goal or dream after all but a fantasy that supports an addiction to the chase.

Manifest your dream, vision, or goal. See it, feel it, breathe it, and live it. You have the power. Spend time each day seeing, feeling, and breathing your dream. See yourself taking steps forward. Feel the joy of accomplishing and living in the dream every day. If you feel fear rise, stop, and take a moment to pinpoint the emotion tied to the fear. Experience it, and let it flow through you. Feel the energy pass through your body, and then let that emotion go. Release that emotion to Mother Earth as you are done with it.

Spend time visualizing each day until you gain clarity about your dream and you are on the path of manifesting. Keep your energy open, saying "yes" to all that is offered or shared with you. Pay attention to places you are saying "no," and assess if they are roadblocks you are creating for yourself. I realize that when I do not obtain a goal, I am overthinking or blocking it myself. The stories or the tapes that run in our heads stop us from reaching the desires or goals we set. Many of those stories have been there for years, and others are newly created. It is time to stop those stories and create a new reality. Begin your new reality by creating it. Just breathe and go!

Exercise

Someday Is Today

Have you talked to trees yet?

What have they said?

Do you believe that they aren't able to answer?

Let go and listen and hear.

The song "Someday" by Rob Thomas talks about hiding and holding all your feelings inside. When we discuss how we hold feelings, we use terms like *internalizing, burying,* or *stuffing.* The first time I heard this song, the line "maybe someday we'll figure out how to live our lives out loud" stuck with me. Hours later, this phrase played over and over in my brain. The next day I heard this song three times within a few hours. No doubt I needed to assess the real message. The reality is that "someday" is now, and the big question is this: am I living out loud?

What does "living out loud" mean? Have you ever felt forgotten, not heard, or invisible? Have you raised your voice without success and given up trying to be heard? Have you found yourself sitting back, silently letting an opportunity pass by? Have you felt cut off or talked over? Have you felt frustrated while allowing someone to monopolize a conversation? These are all signs of not finding your voice. We have all been in these situations, and out of frustration, embarrassment or not feeling valued, we relinquish our power and give up. Many of us have this experience in one or many domains in our life; work, home, school, with family, friends, and loved ones, or with total strangers. If we share similar experiences and feelings, why are *we* sometimes the individual who demonstrates this behavior? Are we not aware when others also feel this way and take action to prevent this?

Having "personal power" often has a bad connotation. Though we have personal power, we give it up, relinquish it, diminish it, hide it, cover it, and don't use it. Power is a gift. It is an enabler for success, action, and manifestation, and it is meant to be used but not abused. Power abuse is when an individual attempts to take another person's power or an individual relinquishes her own power. When you exert your power over someone or attempt to position yourself over another, you diminish both their being and your own power.

Utilize personal power without control and from a place of love. Finding your power can be challenging and frightening. Living out loud means living fully in your power without exerting power over or above someone else. It is acting upon thoughts, words, and feelings without reservation, doubt, or concerns of what people might think. It is living in personal freedom without judgment.

Being in the present and finding your personal power is being in the now. It is all about living out loud. It is about being in the experience and participating in life. If you are not heard or do not make an attempt to be heard, how can you be an active participant? You are a bystander. People with certain communication styles and personality types find it easier to remain in the background, or they relinquish their control and hope that they will have their opportunity next time. The truth is we are all on this earth, in this lifetime, at this moment, at this event to *participate*. If we are not heard and do not attempt to be heard, how do we ever participate? We remain the bystander and our lives watching others.

Living a purposeful life means living as a participant, living in your power, and living out loud. Do not be a silent bystander who relinquishes control. Be loud, be heard, and be fearless. Live out loud, and use your personal power to control your destiny. Breathe and go! Go talk to trees!

Move-Move-Move

If you are not sure that you are on your journey or making progress, don't give up. Move, move, move. It is easy to stop, rest, and *not* start again. Transformation takes energy, and sometimes that energy usage leaves us feeling exhausted. You may even question if the work is good because it's so painful.

It is work to fully understand internal energies, and sometimes pain comes along with that work. A few years ago, I had shirts printed with "Do the Work" and gave them to people who were doing the work and kept doing the work even through painful times. They did not know when they would be done, perhaps never, but they never gave up. When I asked them what motivated them to keep going, they said it was looking back, seeing how far they had come, and the excitement of not knowing how far they had to go. Someday, you will look back over time and realize the huge changes that you have lived along the path.

Believe that you are moving forward on your journey, and remember that it is always easier to look back than it is to look forward. Consider how far you have come since beginning this book.

Exercise

Test Where You Are on the Energy Curve

1. I have attempted meditation.

2. I have kept a journal.

3. I have focused on me and on being versus "getting stuff done."

4. I have talked to trees.

5. I have heard them answer me.

6. I've had cases where I've let go, and in the past, I would not have done this.

7. I have said "yes" to something I've always said "no" to.

If you have done more than four of these actions, you are on your way to understanding your energy and how to use it.

Exercise

Six Questions to Rate Energy

Please answer the following						
	never	2x week	3x week	5x week	7x week	multiple x each day
I find myself smiling for no apparent reason						
I say yes to activities because they will be fun and I WANT to do them						
I have a regular schedule for meals, sleep and exercise						
I look forward to being with people						
I wake ready for a new day						
I look forward to my day						
total						

Scoring

Add each column and multiply the total by the following point value below.

never	-5
2 times per week	1
3 times per week	2
5 times per week	3
7 times per week	4
multiple times each day	5

Analysis

If you have a negative number, you are depleting your energy by these actions and have to work harder to refuel and sustain yourself at a balanced energy level.

Compare this score to your score in chapter 2.

If your score here is greater than when you took the same assessment in chapter 2, you are on your way to awareness and clearing and maintaining your energy levels. If your number is lower, you have more work to do. Remember, when you give out more energy than you are receiving, you become depleted. Stress, lack of sleep, poor nutrition, and poor exercise or no exercise also deplete your energy. Excessive caffeine or other stimulants temporarily give you more energy, but that momentary rush of energy quickly crashed to new lows.

Exercise

I Commit to Myself

I will not expended energy for things that I cannot control or change.

I will be alert and notice all that make me feel energized and things that drain my energy.

When feeling drained, I will leave the situation if I am not able to change it or how I feel about it.

I will surround myself with people that support me, my beliefs, and my goals in life.

I equally share positive energy with others to provide balance in give/take circumstances.

Chapter 9: Living Here

Be Authentic, Be Real

When we no longer desire to live "in the fast lane" and desire to find a more purposeful or soulful presence, we begin to wonder about our purpose. Finding inner peace allows us to live in a different energy each day. This is the higher vibrational energy of joy, peace, love, and fulfillment. We enjoy life instead of feeling we have been run over by a Mack truck. When we find this place, this point of higher vibrational energy, we are being authentic with our true inner soul. We are being real.

You Are Not a Cookie

There is no one else like you. Your thoughts, ideas, beliefs are unique to you. Only you know what your experiences are, and there are no cookie cutter solutions! What is right for someone else is not necessarily right for you. Look inside. Do the hard work of getting to know what is important to you and what is not important. Grant yourself permission to believe it, speak about it, act on it, and create what is right for you.

Being Who You Are Fills the Spirit

Your energy wells become full to a point where you cannot give enough of the energy away! With a steady flow of in-energy, therefore there is a steady flow of out-energy. When you are doing actions that align with who you are and what lights your internal fire, it ignites your passion, and you fill from the work you do. That means you have more to share in all the domains of your life. This sets the stage for life-balance, the balance that sustains us when one domain feels depleted. This is when an overflowing, energized domain can support other the domains until they are back in balance.

Being Who You Are Not Drains the Well

When you are wearing a mask, doing actions that are not in alignment with who you are, you have to dig into your energy reserves to remain energized. This depletes you and eventually drains the well, if not corrected. You can temporarily take reserves from other areas of your life, but this is not sustainable over time.

If you continue to deplete your reserves, eventually you're going to start "pulling up dust from the bottom of the bucket." At this point, your vibrational levels are extremely low and will take healing and time to replenish. For some people, this is where depression, illness and fatigue begin. They describe it as "that sinking feeling." Pay attention to the signs that your body is giving you and the signs that Mother Earth, nature, and your guides are providing.

You Will Never Be Someone Else Half as Well as You Can Be You

Being *you* in all domains of your life means that you function at your core level, in your unique zone. Your vibrations are high, which translates to more energy to use or build upon. You don't have to use up half your energy just to maintain the status quo. Life feels like you are moving with Ease, Elegance, and Excellence—then add Excitement, Entertainment, and Ecstasy:

$$EEE + EEE$$

This is where you are able to manifest your dreams quicker and life feels right.

If Your Situation Stinks Now, More Time Won't Make It Better

Waiting for "things to get better" is not an option. Some may think that waiting is not an action, but when we wait or we do nothing; we are taking action. We are telling spirit that the status quo is okay. If you do not feel good about your relationship, your work, your health, you home, or whatever you are focused on, think about how you will feel in one, three, or five years. The answer is not "better." Ask yourself this: "If I don't do something now, what will tomorrow/next month/next year look like?" Waiting and hoping expend energy and do nothing to fulfill you.

Move, Take Action

Do not sit and wait for the "time to be right." You will throw up roadblocks and false action plans that start with 'I'll start tomorrow" or "next week is better." Why not *now*? If you have gotten to a point of low energy, you know that this situation did not occur five minutes ago. It has been brewing for a while, so why not act now? Even if you cannot take giant leaps toward change, you can take small steps. Consistent, small steps will take you where you want to go far faster than sitting and waiting...and waiting...and waiting.

Multiple Perfect Things Waiting for You

Each person's reasons for loving the exact same thing can be different. Understanding the underlying characteristics of what you love will make it easier to recognize what you specifically want. Incorporate them and live your passion.

Contrary to popular opinion, there isn't one "dream job" that you were meant to do. There are many of them! Being self-aware of what you love provides the foundation to find a perfect job and understand there is more than one option.

There is not one perfect match out there for you, but rather many. We live in a world with over 6.5 billion people. Once you understand who you are and are comfortable with being, you can better define what you look for in a partnership. You are better equipped to draw an equal to you. When your energy levels are different, you attract equal vibrational energies. Good attracts good, and loving attracts loving.

Once you understand the underlying characteristics of your essence you can use them to identify what you want to draw into your life.

Exercise

Pay attention
Be authentic
Listen
Be present, and be aware

Do what you want to do, not what someone else wants you to do or be

Do what feels right, makes you smile and laugh. Be happy and always be in joy.

Just BE!

Living New

Understanding that you have just begun on the journey toward a new way of living or a new way of being, how do you sustain this? I've worked in corporate America for almost thirty years now. Some environments are more structured than others. This book is based on years of false starts, stopped starts, and the final breakthrough.

The breakthrough came when I stopped trying to be something I was not. It was stepping into who my soul was reminding me to be. The moment I acknowledged my gifts and the core person I am, my energy levels rose. My stress left. This is not to say that life did not continue to throw challenges at me. Most recently, I had a month of broken appliances, children situations, relationship challenges, and employee concerns. It *all* seemed to tumble down on the same day! What is different is how I approach these events. I know that I am competent. I know I will be cared for by this planet, and I have the tools to move forward and keep my vibration levels high. There are memories of past moments and dreams of the future, but we only live this moment, so I choose to enjoy this moment. I choose to be in joy this moment. I chose to remain at the highest vibrational level I am able to be at and continue my journey forward.

I have had a prayer for as long as I can remember. I cannot say that I say it daily, but when I practice saying it each day, it reminds me to be present. It reminds me to live and bask in the present moment.

The following prayer for abundance invokes the laws of attraction. It has circulated around the healer and lightworker network for years. Over time, I have modified it to draw clarity and focus to the present moment. During this time of transformation and finding inner peace, may we all find our answers.

Prayer for Abundance

By the powers of the East, which have ably mastered all adversity,
By the Powers of the West, where there are no obstacles to my will,
By the Powers of the North, where luck smiles upon me every day of the year,
By the Powers of the South, where all my desires are immediately granted:

I seek that my life be free from all negative thoughts and actions.
My close family, my friends, my employers and my employees are happy.
My projects, my hopes, my dreams, my business, my work is excellent, fulfilling and fun.
My meals, my food is delicious and healthy.
My water is replenishing and pure.

I don't wish to be younger or older.
I want to benefit ardently from the present hour and the present day.
I am full of kindness for the whole world.
I expect nothing in exchange for the love that I give.

I wish that the abundance, strength, confidence, and attractions born of my thoughts, my words, and my actions flood all of my life and that everything I touch changes into treasure.
I wish that my love from divine be shared with those ready to experience the enormity of the abundance of life.
So note it to be.

Continuing To Be

To continue our energy flow and be at inner peace is to serve and receive. Just as it is important to give of ourselves and share our gifts, it is equally important to receive. When they are out of balance, our energy levels are not sustainable. If you are in a relationship where you are always giving, you deplete the energy reserve in that domain of your life. This keeps you in a lower vibration for your energies. When you are in balance and there is give and take in the relationship (although it may be out of balance at times), there is balance overall. It's a working relationship when one is depleted and the other can provide and vice versa. Find relationships that are balancing and sustaining, not draining. This holds true for a job or career you are in, the home or location you live, and other situations that continually draw on your energy stores.

When our energies are in balance, we are balanced, and we are able to feel our core *BE-ing*. It is easy to fall into old patterns and easy to "stuff" what we are feeling and get back to doing. This is a society that has mastered do-ing but is far behind other areas of the world for *be-ing*. This is about the core inner center of energy that will cry out for sustenance. Once it feels what pure being is about, it will want to return there. This is a good craving and is the soul's reminder of how we are meant to be. It is when we long to know our purpose that our souls send us messages to go within and familiarize ourselves with that inner energy. This is not an exercise in simply reading this book but rather a profound change in how you approach life. You may lose relationships or friendships with these changes. You may leave your job or move to a new home or location. If in alignment with your core, the moves should be with ease and grace. Life is always directing you to live to your higher purpose, and it requires work in the form of awareness and focused practice.

Continue to say "yes" and to stretch yourself beyond what you think your boundaries are.

I will say that again! Stretch yourself beyond what you *think* your boundaries are, which is beyond what you know are your boundaries. When you have the urge to say "no" to something, ask yourself why you are saying no to the opportunity. Look at it as an opportunity. Look at the masks and the walls that you have put up. Look at the fears or other emotions that are tied to saying "no." Are they real or perceived?

Growing It

When you maintain your core energy and are in balance, you can grow this energy. When this energy grows, your vibration levels elevate, and you can connect to a higher self.

Our higher selves hold forms of knowledge and information. When you're at this higher vibration level, you are able to access this information. Many may get to this point but then back away or subdue this gift. In my youth, there were many times I became aware of a gift, intuition, knowing, messaging, dreaming, seeing, and all the other names I gave it over the years. I was afraid that I was different or that people would think I was odd. I masked and hid my core. I became a workaholic, a work-out-aholic, a food-aholic, and circled back through the loop, always burying my real purpose. I saw glimmers but always asked, "Who, me?"

When you step into your purpose, you step into your power. This is acknowledging who you are and letting go of who you are not and who others thought you are supposed to be.

When you see your internal core, life becomes amazingly simple. You are no longer required to hold onto pain or emotions that have no purpose. I still work in corporate America, and I love my job. I have a new awareness of why I am there, my purpose there, and my purpose with my children, family, and friends. I understand that my purpose is to *be* without judgment or pain.

Along my journey, I continually remind myself to *be* as I am. I must also allow everyone else to also find their "I AM" and allow them to *be*.

Containing It

Why would I want to contain this wonderful energy and knowledge that I now have access to? I do not, and you should not either. This is about pulling the knowledge in and using it, not shutting it in a container. It is learning how to access reserves and to share. It is about how to evolve your energies to higher consciousness. It is about awaking your soul, your mind, and your spirit to its higher purpose and higher self. When you find that, share it.

With blessed love!

Reference List

1   Espinoza, Javier. 2011 Energy (A Special Report) --- Earth savings: How to reduce energy consumption, save money and help the environment . *The Wall Street Journal Europe*, April 10.

2   Farmer, Steven. 2006. *Animal Spirit Guides.* Hay House, Inc.

Made in the USA
San Bernardino, CA
22 October 2013